CW01090625

Mini-Beast
A beginner. ⌣

First published 2021

Email: minibeastssafari@yahoo.com

ISBN: 978-1-9164575-8-4

Published by Thomas Curculio

Printed by Panda Press, Stone, Staffordshire

Cover photographs:

Golden-bloomed Grey Longhorn, Agapanthia villosoviridescens (top left)
Juniper Shieldbug, Cyphostethus tristriatus (top right)
Meadow Brown, Maniola jurtina (bottom right)
Scalloped Hook-tip larva, Falcaria lacertinaria (bottom left)

Contents

Part One: Introduction to finding, identifying and recording insects

'Save our bees! We are all doomed if we don't!' This has become the mantra of the conservation movement in recent times. It catches our attention, but it hides a wider issue. All our insects are potentially in trouble. Yet we know precious little about most of them. We can all do something to help remedy this situation. Insects need more than 'bee hotels' to survive into the future. If you want to know what you can do to help, read on.

Introduction

As the author, I am an amateur entomologist with many years of experience. When I am out in the field, I am often stopped by people who have an interest in insects but do not know where to start. They often ask questions about how to find insects, how to identify them or what is the purpose of doing so.

This book is designed to help budding amateur entomologists with the basics. You will gain an insight into the huge variety of insects we have on our own doorsteps. You will learn how to go about finding, identifying and recording insects and how important this is to conservation.

This book is not written by a professional or academic with a reputation to keep. It is written by an amateur for amateurs. There is little in the way of technical language and there are no competition winning photographs that cost fortunes to produce (though there are lots of photos). The intention is not to scare people off with complexity or concerns about expense. Rather, it is to encourage enthusiasts by showing what a mere mortal can achieve at little cost.

The animal kingdom is divided up into several large groups. One of the largest groups is the invertebrates. That just means 'animal without a backbone'. The invertebrate group is then divided into smaller groups. One of these smaller groups is the arthropods. A typical arthropod has its skeleton on the outside (exoskeleton) and a body made up of several segments with jointed legs. This includes crustaceans, arachnids and insects.

Most people are aware of insects: we are surrounded by them, all the time. However, it is the biggest, brightest or easiest to identify that are most often noticed. This is reflected in our knowledge, as shown in distribution maps and atlases. The study of insects is called entomology.

You do not need a special qualification to do some basic entomology. What you need is somewhere to start, some basic know-how. There are many popular field guides to some of our insect families, especially butterflies, moths and bees. These books will allow you to identify some of the most commonly seen and recorded species. They could also lead you to think that we do not have many species of insects in Britain. There are, in fact, around 24 000 different species in the British Isles. Much less than 20% of these insects can be found in popular field guides. The internet does not do much better either.

Most of our basic insect data is now collected by amateur entomologists. If you learn how to do this, you can make a significant contribution to the science and to conservation. If you look at distribution maps for most of our insects, you will get the impression that they are nearly all rare. The truth is that there are simply not enough enthusiasts going out looking for insects and submitting records of their findings. In any county you will be able to find insects that have not yet been recorded. If you find and identify them, you will be in the records as the first person to record them for that area. Every year many species new to Britain are found by amateurs. It is most likely that there are even species completely new to science out there waiting to be discovered.

The life cycles and habits of most of our insects are also poorly or completely unknown. Some of you may want to go beyond recording to do in-depth field research and discover things about insects that no-one yet knows. Gathering new knowledge about the natural world did not start and end with the likes of Gilbert White and Charles Darwin! We have been studying nature for a very long time but still know very little.

The world of insects is fascinating in its sheer variety. It is out there waiting for someone to go and take a look. Watching wildlife on television is fine for cold, wet days. However, there is nothing to beat discovering new things for yourself in real life, out in the wild.

What are insects?

Insects usually have three body segments: a head, a thorax and an abdomen. They usually have three pairs of legs, though sometimes one pair may be modified. If a creature has more than three pairs of legs it is not an insect. Likewise, if a creature has more or less than three body segments it is not an insect. Of course, many of the most familiar insects also have wings but this is not always the case. As you will discover in entomology, for every rule there are many exceptions.

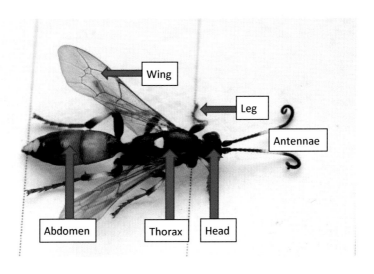

British insects are split into around 558 families in 27 larger groups known as orders. The species in each order all have some common features. The beetles, for example, usually have the front wings modified into hard wing cases called elytra. The true flies have their hind wings modified into halteres which help with balance and give them their amazing flying skills. Most wasps and bees have two normal pairs of wings, though some have none. Thus, an insect can usually be placed in its correct order at a glance using simple features such as these. Identifying an insect beyond family level gets a bit more complicated.

The most visible and well-known orders, in order of size are: Hymenoptera (7000 bees, wasps and ants), Diptera (7000 flies), Coleoptera (4000 beetles), Lepidoptera (2570 butterflies and moths) and Hemiptera (1830 bugs). The remaining insect orders have 250 or fewer species each and many are poorly known and seldom recorded.

A selection of Hymenoptera

Clockwise from top left:
Megachile willoughbiella
Nomada rufipes
Chrysis ignita
Formica fusca
Calameuta pallipes
Habrocampulum biguttatum
Mutilla europaea

6

A selection of Diptera

Clockwise from top left:
Tipula vernalis
Chrysops viduatus
Phasia hemiptera
Cheilosia albitarsis
Physocephela rufipes
Campiglossa malaris
Neria cibaria

A selection of Coleoptera

Clockwise from top left:
Carabus problematicus
Dendroxena quadrimaculata
Ctenicera cuprea
Glischrochilus hortensis
Stenocorus meridianus
Cassida vibex
Apodemus coryli

A selection of Lepidoptera

Clockwise from top left:
Polyommatus icarus
Maniola jurtina
Zygaena filipendulae
Zeuzera pyrina
Eurrhypara hortulata
Pyrausta aurata
Malacosoma neustria

A selection of Hemiptera

Clockwise from top left:
Eurygaster testudinaria
Corizus hyoscyami
Metatropis rufescens
Himacerus apterus
Oncopsis flavicollis
Centrotus cornutus
Hydrometra stagnorum

Insects from some smaller orders

Clockwise from top left:
Sympetrum striolatum. Odonata,
Damselflies and Dragonflies.

Tetrix ceperoi. Orthoptera,
Grasshoppers and Crickets.

Crysopa perla. Neuroptera, Green
Lacewings.

Ephemera danica. Ephemeroptera,
Mayflies.

Orchesella cincta. Collembola,
Springtails.

Petrobius maritimus. Thysanura,
Bristletails.

It has become commonplace to use the term 'bugs' for all insects. Technically this is incorrect, only the insects of the Hemiptera are bugs. So, be careful when the word 'bugs' is used, some bugs are more bug than others!

This book is mainly about insects, but the principles apply equally well to all other invertebrate groups. They are all worthy of studying and recording. Slugs and snails, for example, are molluscs. They are invertebrates as they have no backbone, but they are not insects as they have no legs. Spiders are arachnids, they always have eight legs and two body segments. Centipedes are isopods with many body segments and numerous pairs of legs.

A selection of non-insect invertebrates

Garden Snail
Cornu aspersum

Molluscs are invertebrates with no legs.

Sand Dune Spider
Arctosa perita

Arachnids are invertebrates with eight legs.

Variegated Centipede
Lithobius variegatus

Isopods are invertebrates with many pairs of legs.

Where do we find insects?

The answer to this question seems quite simple: wherever we choose to look! However, if you want to find specific types of insects, then you need to find out where they prefer to live. Some insects are not fussy and can survive in a range of habitats. These tend to be the species we see all the time, in our gardens or local green spaces. Most people have seen, for example, insects such as Large White Butterfly, 7-spot Ladybird or Common Wasp.

Most species, however, are quite choosey about where they live and often have very specific requirements. There are, for example, several beetle species that only live in dead wood infected by certain fungi in ancient oak forests. This habitat is in rather short supply in Britain, so these species are rare and hard to find.

It might seem that the obvious place to start would be to buy some books or to look on the internet. In my experience the best way to learn is to go outside and read the natural environment. This is how I learned, the books came later, when I had become interested enough to justify the cost. There are specialist books out there, but many are quite expensive. They are not the kind of books to be left on shelves gathering dust having never been read. This is why they tend not to turn up in charity shops. The people who buy them use them and keep them!

As a beginner it is probably best to look for a range of species in a range of different habitats. This way you can find a variety of interesting insects and get a sense of what a habitat is all about. If you target the larger more colourful species, they are more likely to be identifiable. They are also easier to handle! As your experience grows you can look for smaller and more obscure species.

You may find that your interest is in all insects and so become what is known as a 'generalist'. Or you may find that certain groups of insects are of more interest to you, then you become a 'specialist'. A 'coleopterist', for example, studies beetles. The best way to find where your interest lies is to take a broad look at the whole invertebrate spectrum. So, where do we find a good variety of species? The best way to start is to look at large-scale 'macro-habitats'.

Macro-habitats

A woodland is a good example of a macro-habitat. It is a large area principally made up of trees. Heathland is a macro-habitat often covered with heathers. Few people would think about their own homes in wildlife terms, but your house is a type of macro-habitat! It may not have the diversity of a forest, but it will be home to a number of insect species and a few other invertebrates.

Insects at Home

Quite a few insects prefer to live indoors. Some have followed humans into houses and outbuildings because we used to share their natural cave habitats. Others, often found in greenhouses or large, warm buildings are 'naturalised' species. These are species imported from warmer parts of the world and cannot survive outdoors in our climate. Many of our cockroaches, for example, are in this category.

There are a number of fly species that prefer to live indoors all year round. You may also have beetles that live in wood or stored food products. If you have woodlice in your house or outbuildings you may find large beetles that specialise in killing them! There will be moths that eat clothes and carpets. There may be silverfish in your pantry and firebrats around your fireplace. At night, a variety of species, including moths, midges and drain flies will be attracted to lights in windows. In the winter, your home and outbuildings may be a refuge for hibernating butterflies and ladybirds.

Other invertebrates such as spiders are common in houses. If you have spiders in your house do not put them outside, as people often do. They are in your house because it is their habitat. They will be killing and eating thousands of insects, including food pests and flies that annoy and bite. Putting house spiders outside could mean death for them.

Gardens and Parks

Gardens and parks are probably the nearest and most convenient outdoor habitats to go on a mini-beast safari. Most of our common butterflies and many colourful hoverflies can be found in these habitats. If there are trees, shrubs or areas where the vegetation looks untidy then there will be a good range of insects. Many of our moth larvae and bugs live on the foliage of trees and shrubs. These in turn become food for predatory and parasitic insects. Whilst many bugs are vegetarian, some attack other insects literally sucking them dry.

A large number of Hymenoptera are parasitic and lay eggs in larvae. These eggs hatch and eat the caterpillar from inside while it is still alive! Take a close look at any foliage in your garden or park and you will find insects you did not know existed. You might also possibly witness the origins of many well-known horror and sci-fi stories!

Buathra laborator, a parasitic wasp

Farmland

Farmland is mostly fields and hedgerows and is by far the most extensive habitat in Britain. At first glance it looks green enough but much of it is of little use to native wildlife, including insects. However, a closer look will reveal interesting species. Take a walk along a hedgerow, preferably one that has not been cut recently and you could find some really good mini-beasts. I have found several species new to our county just by walking along the country lane outside our house! Before there was farmland most of Britain was woodland. When humans removed the native woodlands, the wildlife had to adapt or die. Many of the birds we associate with hedgerows are in fact woodland birds. The same is true for insects, many of them have survived by adapting to our hedgerows.

The average field of wheat or barley will be inhospitable to most insects. This is due to the lack of wildflowers and the toxicity of agricultural sprays. Grazing meadows can be better places to look. We have a good range of species associated with grasslands and animal dung. There are numerous fly species associated with large animals such as cows and horses. Some of our most notorious biting flies, horseflies and cleggs, can be found around paddocks and farmyards. These flies can be spectacular with iridescent eyes and patterned wings.

There is likely to be a better range of wild plants in a grazing meadow attracting a bigger variety of insects. The grasses and low plants, such as clovers, will be host to numerous species. A number of butterflies, moths and sawflies will lay eggs on grasses, especially those with broad leaf blades and in areas where the grass has grown rough. These larvae, in turn, attract parasites and predators. Tall flowering plants, such as white Cow Parsley and yellow Ragwort will attract all sorts of flies, bees and bugs. Even some of our larger parasitic wasps can be seen taking nectar from these plants on sunny days.

Woodland

Take a walk through the average conifer plantation and the lack of wildlife is deafeningly obvious. This is because the trees are most often non-native; our insects are not evolved to use them. Those insects found in such places are often conifer specialists. The Larch Sawfly larva, for example, feeds on the needles of the European Larch.

Pristiphora laricis, a sawfly that lives only on Larch.

A number of beetle and sawfly larvae tunnel in the trunks of coniferous trees. They leave obvious exit holes when they emerge as adults. Wood ants build large conical nests using pine needles. These can look quite spectacular dotted around a bare forest floor. Take a closer look and you will see that they are crawling with ants. You may even be lucky enough to spot an ant mimic. There are a number of species ranging from beetles, bugs and even spiders that resemble ants.

Sadly, in Britain, we destroyed most of our native woodlands a long time ago. Only fragments of the ancient forest exist. They are special places and, thankfully, most are now protected. Most of our broad-leaved woodland has been planted in more recent times. The trees still provide habitats for our largest ranges of insect species. The

Brocton Coppice. A fragment of ancient woodland

larger and older the trees the more variety you will find. Oak trees have the largest number of associated insects. This was only surpassed by elm trees, but you are truly fortunate if you have large mature elms growing near you.

Pyrochroa serraticornis

Beetle larvae such as this Pyrochroa serraticornis are commonly found under the bark of dead or dying trees. Other species will tunnel through the wood or between the layers of bark. Their tunnels can often be seen as patterns called 'galleries'.

16

The foliage of broadleaved trees is alive with insects from the opening of the first buds until the last leaf falls. Expect to find a large variety of insects from many different families. The most numerous are usually the aphids. They are small and appear to the eye to be uninteresting. However, we have around 650 species, many of which are quite colourful and richly patterned. Most aphids go unrecorded, yet they are a rather important link in the food web. They attract lots of other insects to the trees, especially predatory ladybirds and their larvae.

Plocamaphis flocculosa

Aphids are small to very small bugs. They can be found on most types of plants. Many of them use different plants at different times of the year and at different stages of their life cycles. Most of them have winged and wingless forms. This Plocamaphis flocculosa was found on Sallow.

'Galls' are growths on plants caused by insects and other invertebrates. Some can be quite large and obvious, many are small and over-looked. The main gall causing groups are gall wasps, gall midges and gall mites (related to spiders). The foliage of trees is particularly prone to attack by gall causing wasps and midges. These insects are often small and inconspicuous, many of them are seldom seen and difficult to identify. However, the galls they cause are often obvious. Most gall causers can be identified and recorded from their galls.

Some galls form on the leaves, like these Cynips quercusfolii, and are fairly easy to spot. Others can form on buds or twigs and are often less obvious. Look for unusual swellings or other growths. If the insects have left, their exit holes may make the galls easier to spot.

Cynips quercusfolii

Water and Wetlands

There are many kinds of habitat that have a water component. These range from temporary pools formed from rainwater to our lakes and rivers. Some of the best wet habitats for insect variety are flood meadows and the vegetated edges of various water bodies. I have found manmade wet habitats to be as good as natural ones. Disused sand and gravel pits, for example, can be quite productive. Patches of gravel at the edges of lakes in quarries can yield a fine array of species. However, quarries are dangerous places and care is needed when searching in such areas.

Near rivers and lakes, look for areas that flood on a regular basis and have a good variety of plant life. Ideally, there should be a good mix of grasses and herbage blending into sedges, rushes and reeds with a scattering of willows and Alder. There is a good variety of insect life to be found in this type of wet habitat. There will be beetles, bugs, the larvae of moths and sawflies and a whole array of other wetland species. In particular look out for caddisflies and mayflies along with the more familiar dragonflies and damselflies.

Do not forget that many insects live in the water. There can be a good variety of both bugs and beetles in the right aquatic habitat. Still water with shallow margins overgrown with sedges, reeds and mats of pond weed or green algae are often the best places to look. I find that water with few or no fish will produce the most insects. Stagnant, water filled ditches will also be good places to look. Some of our largest beetles prefer stagnant waters.

Alderflies like this Sialis lutaria have aquatic larvae.

Dragonflies, damselflies and many other flying insects have larvae that live in water. In many cases these larvae can be identified and recorded. Some of these larvae feed on detritus and algae. Some are predators of other insects. Large dragonfly larvae can even catch and eat small fish!

There are other, more specialised, wet habitats. Peat bogs and lowland wet mires are often acidic. The insects that live in such places are adapted to this kind of environment and often will not live anywhere else. Such habitats are not common in lowland England. There are some good sites in Dorset, Shropshire and Cheshire in particular. Otherwise, you would need to go to the uplands of Wales or Scotland.

Even the smallest bodies of water can hold aquatic insects. Some small water beetles will live in temporary rain puddles such as water filled tyre ruts. However, with any water body keep an eye open for pollution as this is likely to reduce or even wipe out any aquatic life. It could also make the water toxic for humans. There is a difference between 'stagnant' and 'polluted' water! Sadly, the water filled rut to the right is polluted as indicated by the presence of rainbow coloured films floating on top. Not all pollution is this obvious. Keep an eye open for other signs such as dead fish. Though, a bad smell will often mean stagnant rather than polluted.

With any water body be aware of the potential danger to yourself, especially if you are not a swimmer. Even the most innocuous bit of a pond can turn out to be deeper than it looks. It is quite easy to slip on wet vegetation and take an unexpected early bath. Many of our rivers and man-made water bodies have steep sides and can be particularly dangerous. Be especially cautious around water outlets/inlets such as locks and sluices as these can create extremely dangerous under-currents. If you are not sure of how safe it is, the best thing is to keep away.

Heathlands

Emperor Moth
Saturnia pavonia

Most of our heathlands formed after man cleared the forests. There are many heathland specialists in the insect world. Many of them are as rare as the habitats they live in. Heathlands are often dominated by Heather. This is a woody and not very palatable plant. It is one the favourite foods of the colourful Emperor Moth larva.

Look out also for the Heather Ladybird and the Heather Bug. The Heather Bug is a predator, eating the larvae of leaf beetles. Prey species are usually quite numerous, but predator populations are often much smaller.

Other macro-habitats

It is a general rule that the greater the range of plant life, the greater the range of insects. This means that flower-rich grasslands can be as productive as native woodlands. These tend to be areas that have not been ploughed or sprayed in an awfully long time, if ever. Much of this habitat has been lost. There are some larger areas in places like the Cotswolds or the Derbyshire Dales and there is a scattering of smaller wildflower meadows elsewhere. Most of these are now nature reserves.

Phillopedon plagiatum, a sand dune weevil

If you live near the coast, then you may have access to some other special habitats. Sand dunes, especially large areas, with good growths of Marram Grass and wildflowers will provide a good range of insects. Many of these will be sand dune specialists. Some of our best dune systems are nature reserves, such as Formby Dunes and Morfa Harlech.

The same is true for saltmarshes. These are quite harsh places for anything to live in. The vegetation is adapted to cope with the high salt levels and insects have adapted to utilise these plants. The plants and many of the insects are often saltmarsh specialists that do not live in any other habitat.

In the north and west of Britain we have large areas of 'uplands'. The habitats in these uplands are often similar to lowland habitats. There are woodlands, grasslands, wetlands etc. They differ mainly because the higher altitude usually means the weather is different. The temperature is on average cooler, winter is a little longer and summer a little shorter. It is also generally wetter. This has an impact on the plant life which in turn determines the insect species that can live there. Many of the lowland species can be found, though often in smaller numbers, and there will be species that only live in the uplands. Generally, the higher up you go, the fewer species you will find.

Brownfield Sites

Brownfield sites are plots of land that have been used by humans for various purposes but have fallen out of use. They can be sites where individual houses once stood or places where large factories have been demolished, for example. They might appear to be places where wildlife could not thrive. In fact, the opposite is true. In recent times it has become apparent that brownfield sites are quite important for wildlife. This is especially true in large urban areas. These places will yield a wide range of insects and other invertebrates.

Some brownfield sites are obvious, they will have visible remains of their past use. This is particularly true of old factory sites in rundown industrial areas. Such sites are quite often dangerous for all sorts of reasons. They are also, usually, still owned by someone and therefore inaccessible. These places can be really good for invertebrates, but you need permission to access them and, if granted, it will most likely be at your own risk. I would not encourage anyone to visit such sites without a lot of careful consideration.

Large brownfield sites, such as quarries and opencast coal mines, are re-landscaped after use and become less obvious. These places are often made accessible as public open spaces or even country parks. They are generally safer, but the diversity will take some years to increase after the re-landscaping has been completed. Sand and gravel quarries will become havens for wildlife fairly quickly. They are particularly interesting if ponds have been created to add to the range of habitats. However, opencast coal sites and the spoil heaps from deep coal mining are always poorer places. They are still worth a look, but do not expect more than you find!

This aggregate quarry was re-landscaped about 20 years ago. It was a rather large hole with steep cliffs and filled with quicksand, but it is now a thriving and rapidly developing habitat. The soil chemistry is the same as what was on the surface before the quarry was dug. This means it has been easy for life to return and re-colonise the site.

This area was a black and grey mountain of spoil from a deep coalmine. These spoil heaps are generally quite toxic and take decades of weathering to make them suitable for plants to thrive. The first attempts to re-landscape this one took place over 40 years ago. The habitat is still a long way behind the quarry shown above.

Micro-habitats

As you become familiar with your local macro-habitat you will learn to recognise maybe a couple of dozen insect species that are seen regularly. These will be the ones that are more visible, usually brightly coloured, easy to spot and easy to identify. You will see them over and over again. They tend to be fairly common species with broad habitat requirements. These insects are spotted and recorded all the time, and this is reflected in their distribution maps.

The key to finding a larger variety of species is to look at smaller 'micro-habitats'. This may sound a bit contradictory, but it makes perfect sense to an entomologist. Most species have rather specific needs, and this usually means that the habitats they live in are quite small. Each species will live in a discreet, specific, part of the macro-habitat. Think of a macro-habitat as being made up from almost countless and distinct micro-habitats.

It is often said that to be a better entomologist you need to be familiar with wild plants. You need to be a good botanist! Almost every type of plant has insects associated with it at some stage of its life cycle. To turn this around, look closely at every plant species in a macro-habitat and you will find a larger range of insect species. Many insects live only on one type of plant. Some plants have a small number of associated species, some have a large number. Thus, each plant species is, in effect, a micro-habitat. Oak trees have already been mentioned. Willows, Silver Birch, bramble patches and beds of Common Nettle also produce good numbers of insect species.

Not all insects are associated with wildflowers or even anything that is alive. Dung, especially horse and cow, is a productive micro-habitat. I use a two-pronged gardening implement to poke around in dung, but a stick is just as good. If you are a little squeamish you can always wear gloves.

It might sound a bit distasteful, but it is not as bad as it seems. It is possible to find a dozen beetle species in one piece of dung, including some of our largest. Of course, you cannot talk about dung without mention of flies! Yellow Dung-flies along with many other Diptera can often be seen swarming over cowpats. Many of them look the same but catch a sample and you will find numerous species among them.

A good number of interesting species are associated with dead animals. I came across a roadkill badger not far from my house. I simply moved it off the road and put it out of sight. After a couple of weeks quite a lot of interesting species started turning up. In all ten species of beetle, only one of which I had seen before, visited the carcass over the course of two months. Of course, it also attracted numerous flesh-eating fly species.

Creophilus maxillosus, a carrion specialist

Dead wood is another good micro-habitat. There are numerous species of insects that live under the bark of trees or in the wood itself. It is not a good idea to try pulling bark off living trees. This could lead to the death of the tree and in most cases it may be illegal! Look for dead trees and try peeling off small sections of bark. There will be different species depending on how long the tree has been dead and the types of fungi that have been involved in the rotting process. The best variety of species will be found under the bark of trees that have only recently fallen and have clearly been infected by fungi for some time. The bark will be tightly fixed to the tree and sap will still be present.

Tree sap and the rot processes make this habitat wet and sticky. You should find wood boring beetles and their larvae, often in the bark, along with species that prey on them. Some of the beetles that live in this micro-habitat are rather flat, an adaptation to this environment. You might also find a few species of bugs and springtails.

The loose dry bark on long-dead trees is usually home to several ground beetle and rove beetle species. Break open old rotten logs for longhorn beetles and click beetles. Some click beetle larvae are predators of other insects living in dead wood. The commonest species to find here, however, is not an insect but a wood louse. In the winter you will find beetles, bugs, ichneumon wasps and even hornets hibernating under loose bark or in rotten wood.

Carabus granulatus, hibernating in dead wood

Try looking under stones or logs for ground beetles. Search among large rotten fungi for a variety of fungus specialists. Look between the leaves of bulrushes or break open the stems of Cow Parsley or Hogweed for bugs, moth larvae, small rove beetles and earwigs. Search leaf litter for small beetles and springtails. Sift through tussocks of grass or moss in winter for hibernating insects. Basically, look everywhere. Every bit of a macro-habitat is a potential micro-habitat with its own species of insects. This is the key to finding a larger variety of British insect life. Think small, less is more!

Insects see things in habitats that we do not fully understand. You can walk along hundreds of metres of hedgerow and find hardly anything. Then, all of a sudden, a few metres of the same hedgerow will come alive with insects. The habitat looks the same to our eyes but is clearly different to them. The same thing can happen in any kind of habitat. It can be off putting if you seem to be walking for hours and finding nothing. Patience and perseverance are required. Just keep going, keep looking and you will find many species. As time goes by, you will develop an eye for a good habitat. Then your searches will become more productive and less frustrating.

Creating Habitats in the Garden

Gardens are a major macro-habitat. However, many gardens are too tidy to attract a great variety of wildlife. Lots of people have birdfeeders and nest boxes but not many would consider inviting 'bugs' into their gardens. No matter how small a garden is, it is not too difficult to create a range of micro-habitats for insects.

Wildflowers are a big attraction for a range of insects, not just the obvious bees and butterflies. We dug up a small strip of lawn and sowed a £1 box of so-called wildflower seeds. They were not genuine wildflowers but garden derivatives. However, they bloomed for eight months and were alive with all sorts of insects. We had, for £1 and a bit of work, a spectacular display that gave many months of pleasure and interest. We even had Orange-tip butterflies breeding in our flower bed!

If you do not have a lawn to dig up, try tubs or window boxes. The smallest growth of wildflowers will attract insects. Remember, it is illegal to remove most native wildflowers from their habitats. So, if you prefer to grow genuine native species then buy them from a licensed supplier. They cost a bit more than the £1 box we first used but they are worth it, and many will self-seed.

Other micro-habitats can be created by leaving piles of dead wood, leaflitter or grass cuttings under a hedge or in a shady spot. These will provide a refuge for a range of species all year round. Try filling 10 litre paint tubs with sand and bury them in a sunny border. These will attract a number of solitary wasp and bee species. They dig small nesting holes in the sand. Watch for the wasps taking caterpillars down the holes.

If you have space, plant native shrubs such as Common Hawthorn or Blackthorn. These will provide food for numerous moth species. Do not trim the hedges too often, though. A garden pond is always a boost for wildlife. It does not need to be big or deep. As long as it is not allowed to dry out for long periods it will provide a home for insects. Even some of the largest of our dragonflies will breed in garden ponds. Basically, look around at natural micro-habitats and think about how you can replicate them in your garden.

Some of the more productive habitats will be covered in more detail in Part 2. There we will discover some of the wonderful diversity to be found in each of them.

A Word on Ecosystems

As you get to know a particular habitat, you will notice that certain species tend to live there in preference to anywhere else. In fact, you will notice that a given habitat will be home to a whole collection of species, each in its own little niche. There will also be certain types of plants and fungi etc. You are looking at an 'eco-system'. An eco-system is a habitat, all of its inhabitants, the local climate and geology and the interactions between all of these things.

All the insects, plants and everything else in an eco-system are linked in some way. Fungi, for example, break down dead leaves and pass nutrients to trees via their roots. Some insects eat green leaves and are then eaten by other insects or spiders. Some birds and mammals spread the seeds of trees and other plants. There are countless interactions and interconnections between species and between them and their environment. These all form, maintain and define the eco-system.

The study of eco-systems comes under 'ecology'. This can be the study of the ecology of a single species or an entire system. There is a great deal we do not know about the ecology of individual species and whole systems are little understood. This is a potentially rewarding area for anyone who wants to develop their interest further.

The idea of conserving wildlife has been around for a long time now. In the early days efforts tended to be focused on conserving individual species. Why do you think the logo of the RSPB is the Avocet? Fund-raising advertising still gives this image, it is always 'Save the ...... something or other'. However, in recent times it is has become more apparent that individual species cannot be saved so easily.

We now know that whole habitats and healthy ecosystems are necessary to keep individual species alive. We cannot hope to keep tigers alive in the wild without saving large areas of natural habitat full of prey. The tiger's prey species have their needs too. The ecosystem has to be healthy and thriving for all the individual species to survive. The same is true closer to home. We cannot save our owls if we do not save the rodents they eat. Those rodents need thriving ecosystems to support their populations. One of the key measures of a healthy, thriving ecosystem is the insect diversity it supports. Insect diversity is monitored, in large part, by amateur entomologists simply going out and recording insects. Exactly what this book is about!

Catching insects

Most insects cannot be identified without catching them. There are numerous ways to catch insects, some better than others, some more specialised than others. As a beginner some basic kit is essential. You will need some type of net and lots of collecting pots to put your specimens in. A hand lens is essential. A tray is useful to empty in the contents of your net and a pair of tweezers or a 'pooter' for handling small specimens. You might also want to carry a killing jar and killing fluid and an implement for searching dung or digging in wood and soil.

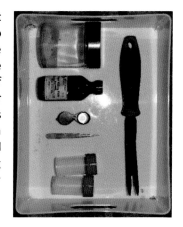

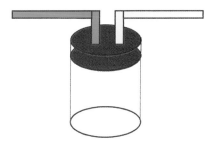

A pooter is a jar with a bunged top. There are two tubes sticking through the bung. One is usually a long rubber tube. The end of the long tube is put close to a specimen and you suck through the other tube. The insect will drop into the jar. These are useful for tiny specimens that would otherwise be difficult to pick up.

Like most of the kit you will use, a pooter can be bought or made. I personally do not use one. I simple moisten a fingertip and insects will stick to it long enough to drop into a pot. I find it quicker and it is one less piece of kit to carry. Though it is not recommended for dung beetles!

Some of the most commonly used techniques for catching insects are 'sweeping', 'beating', 'sieving' and 'dipping'. These are explained below.

Sweeping

Many people start out with a butterfly net. This is fine if you only want to catch butterflies or other large flying insects. If you want to catch a bigger variety, you need a sweep net. Sweep nets come in a number of styles and sizes. The main point about them is that they are tough enough to be swept through vegetation.

Sweep nets usually have a rigid frame with a hard-wearing material for the net bag. They will work well in most types of vegetation. I have several nets that were purchased ready-made. However, I have just made one from a discarded fisherman's landing net, with extending handle, and a bit of leftover net curtain. The netting is densely woven and quite tough. This net cost next to nothing and half an hour to make!

From left to right:

Standard butterfly net

Pocket net, frame folds up to fit in pocket. Also has a telescopic handle.

Sweep net with heavy duty bag.

Smaller sweep net with light-weight bag

Simply make a number of sweeps with the net and see what you catch. Take wide sweeps making sure the net gets down into the vegetation. Try to avoid sweeping through too much bramble or other thorny plants. When you stop sweeping, let the net twist or hang over the frame to stop everything escaping before you see what you have caught. There will usually be a good number of different insects and other invertebrates. If you do not like spiders, best not look in the net!

Pot up the specimens you are interested in and release the rest. If you are interested if flying insects, it is best to get them in pots quickly before they disappear! I find that flies will escape the quickest followed by bees and wasps. Other Hymenopterans, such as ichneumons, tend to be calmer and will often sit in the net for a while. Many beetles and shieldbugs will try to climb out of the net. Other types of bugs and flea beetles will more likely jump out. With  experience, you will quickly spot and catch the specimens you are most interested in and ignore the rest. Always catch the ones you want the most first! If you are not interested in the flying insects, you can tip the contents of the net into a tray.

In most good bits of habitat, it is worth sweeping the air around about you and above your head. There are many thousands of insects in the air around us most of the time. We just tend not to notice most of them, unless they are big wasps or biting flies. You should be able catch many different insects in flight. Your sweep net will be good enough or you can use a butterfly net with a wider diameter for a bigger catch.

Beating

Sweep nets are not so good for trees and shrubs or anything with thorns that will entangle and tear the net. If you are looking for insects in thorny bushes, for example, you need a beating tray and a stick. It is possible to use your net as a tray and the handle as a stick. Simply hold the tray under some branches and tap them with the stick. Insects and their larvae will be dislodged and land in the tray. You will catch plenty of slower insects such as bugs and moth larvae. Sadly, most of the Diptera and Hymenoptera will  quickly disappear. There is not much you can do about this unless you have someone standing by with a net.

A large-scale version of beating involves the use of a sheet. The idea is to place a large sheet, preferably white, on the ground under a tree or bush. Then beat the branches with a suitable stick. Remember though, you only want to find insects. The intention is not to cause fatal damage to the tree! Also, watch for branches flicking back and catching your eyes.

Sieving

Organic debris, such as leaf litter, grass cuttings or rotted wood, is often teaming with invertebrate life. Most of the insects found in such habitats are quite small, many of them much less than 3mm long. These insects can be difficult to spot in their habitat. So, entomologists use 'sieving' methods to extract them and make them more visible.

How you go about sieving depends, partly, on the amount of kit you want to carry around. A common method involves a builders bucket and a garden sieve. The idea is to sieve plenty of litter over the bucket to separate out all of the larger debris.

Smaller debris and, hopefully, lots of insects will fall through the sieve into the bucket to be sorted through. If you prefer, bags of litter can be taken home to sieve. This leaves more of your time for collecting. I found some cheap plastic trays just the right size for my 70L backpack. I cut the bottom out of one and replaced it with a piece of wire mesh. This works perfectly well and cost a few pounds. There are commercially produced products available.

After the initial sieving, you could try using a mesh with smaller holes. Or you could just search through the sieved material by eye and pick up specimens with a pooter. Alternatively, the sieved material can be placed in sealed bags and taken home to look through later. If you take the material home it can be put into an extractor device. These can be purchased or homemade. The basic idea is to let the insects sieve themselves out of the debris leaving you time to deal with anything else collected on the same trip.

Before spending lots of money on readymade extractors try making a simple device from plastic bottles. Take two large pop bottles. Cut one approximately in half. The bottom half needs to be blacked-out with tape or paint as this will be the collecting chamber. Cut the bottom section off the other one, just above where the plastic starts to curve. Drill some holes in one of the lids, about 4 or 5mm diameter should do.

Leaf litter is put into the second bottle and the bottom put on as a cap to stop anything escaping that way. Leave the drilled screw cap on. This is then pushed into the blacked-out half of the first bottle. Insects in the litter will naturally move out of the light of the upper part and down into the dark of the collector. I have tried this, and it works well enough. If you like the idea you can make better devices or buy one off the shelf.

Of course, what comes out of the extractor will depend on your leaf litter sample. Expect to find small beetles, including ground and rove beetles, ground bugs, springtails and hoverfly larvae. There will also be woodlice and spiders. You may even be lucky enough to find some pseudoscorpions. These tiny predators look like miniature scorpions. They are not

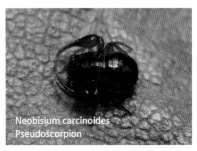
Neobisium carcinoides
Pseudoscorpion

insects but arachnids. They have eight legs, the same as the spiders to which they are related. They are hard to spot. They often sit perfectly still and run backwards when disturbed! Check your device regularly or you may end up with just one fat predator!

Dipping

If you do not want to buy, or to carry, too much kit you can use your sweep net in the water too. There are pond dipping nets available, the main difference is in the material of the net bag. It is usually coarser to let the water out more quickly. A child's fishing net will do. It will catch most of the larger species but some of the smallest will escape. They do not last long but they are usually cheap to replace. You can either pot specimens straight from the net or tip the contents into a tray. The tray needs to be deep enough to stop specimens running or jumping straight back into the pond!

Do not forget to sweep the vegetation while you are there. Lots of insects live in tall waterside plants such as Common Reed and Bulrush. Best not use a wet net for sweeping though. Many insects have delicate wings that are spoilt if the net is wet.

Other than the methods described above, there are several commonly used types of trap. Pitfall traps will catch species that run about on the ground. Simply dig a pit and place in it a container; a tin or plastic paint pot will do. If you want the insects alive put small holes in the bottom for rainwater to drain out. You can place a cover over the top, such as a piece of wood or stone, but leave a gap for insects to go under and fall in. Check the trap regularly as some species

will eat others and you may not get the full potential out of the trap.

A simple, cheap pitfall trap can be made with a plastic bottle. Cut the bottle in half. Bury the bottom half in the ground. Make sure the soil goes right up to the edge so that insects will drop in.

Cover the trap with a piece of wood or tile propped up in each corner with a stone or soil. Leave it for at least a few days before checking. This method works, I have tried it. It is a good place for a beginner to start. Later you can experiment with other, perhaps larger, containers. Pitfall traps can also be baited. Try bits of cheese, meat or fish.

If you get more serious, you might want to try malaise traps or emergence traps. Each will catch a different and varied range of species. They can be purchased ready-made or you can make your own. Bear in mind that any trap should be inspected regularly so as not to kill and waste lots of insects unnecessarily.

Suction Sampling

The most productive method, by far, for obtaining ground dwelling species is the 'suction sampler'. It seems a bit extreme, but it works really well and is growing in popularity. To do this you need a garden vac or blower/vac. A battery powered model will be lighter to carry and you do not have to take cans of fuel in addition. Fasten a net bag into to the suction tube to catch the insects which are then tipped into a tray. I have seen this method turn up dozens of species in one go.

This model is a blower/vac.

A simple net is made and taped into the tube.

There are more tubes, but I prefer the length shown.

This model also has a power control. On full power the battery will last for half an hour of continuous use.

As it will be used in short bursts it should do for most of a day.

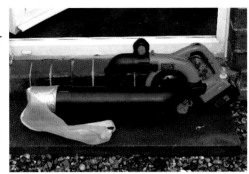

Mothing

As with much of your kit, moth traps can be bought or home-made. A key component is the light source which is most often a UV tube, actinic bulb or a mercury vapour bulb. The latter are now being phased out, due to changes in the law, but are still available. Obviously, moth traps are most commonly used by moth enthusiasts. However, there are many other nocturnal insects that will come to a light. You can expect beetles, bugs, flies and parasitic Hymenopterans. It is surprising what will turn up. I have had dung beetles, water beetles, water bugs and nocturnal Hymenoptera in my moth trap in a single session.

There are a number of different types of trap available. This one is a 'Skinner' trap. The main difference between traps is how efficient they are at holding on to the catch. A good supplier, such as Natural History Book Service (NHBS), will provide information on how well each type of trap works. Only certain species are attracted to light. No matter what kind of trap you use only those attracted to light will be caught. All other species have to be found using other techniques. This will be discussed further in Part 2.

Grow Your Own Insects

All insects have several life stages. Most species lay eggs or 'ova'. Some, especially bugs, can give birth to live young. The juvenile stages can be 'grubs', 'larvae' or 'nymphs'. Most fly eggs hatch into legless grubs, often known as maggots. The eggs of butterflies, moths and beetles hatch into larvae. Larvae usually have legs. The eggs of bugs hatch into nymphs. Nymphs usually resemble the adult bugs but without wings.

The exoskeletons of insects are hard and cannot expand. However, all the larval stages must go through several growth spurts known as 'instars'. The larvae feed for a period of time, then stop for a while to change the skin. The old skin splits and is discarded. The new skin underneath is soft and expands to a larger size before setting hard. In many species the larvae can look different after each instar is completed. The last instar turns into a pupa which hatches into the adult. All insects have their own version of this basic pattern.

It is quite often possible to identify insect larvae. This is particularly true of moths, butterflies and sawflies. You can collect and rear larvae in order to obtain adult insects. This is rather useful if you want to photograph fresh adult specimens. The key thing is to know what the larvae eat and make sure you can provide this before collecting them. Often it is simply a case of identifying the foodplant and having a nearby supply.

Larvae can be kept in any kind of small container. They must be safe from predators and parasites but also have ventilation. Most food types should be changed every day or two, especially soft leaves that will wither and dry out quickly. It is important to keep the containers clean and keep them out of direct sunlight.

The container on the right has a piece of kitchen towel in the bottom to soak up excess moisture. It also catches the frass (caterpillar poo) making it easier to clean out. Either use the original lid with small holes drilled in it or cover with a piece of net to allow air to circulate. Most larvae can be kept safely together in small numbers. Overcrowding will most likely lead to failure.

Beware, some larvae are predatory and even cannibalistic! Individual larvae can be kept in smaller containers if necessary. All containers should be labelled with species, date and location where collected.

Once pupation has taken place, pupae can be kept in an emergence cage like the one shown here. There are many different styles and sizes available.

Individual pupae should be labelled to keep track of your specimens. This is useful for several reasons. Most of our butterflies and moths are hosts for parasitic wasps. Some of these will emerge from your pupae. It is then important to record the parasite and the host species. Labels can be glued to the tail end of pupae with a spot of wood glue.

There are a number of moths and beetles with larvae that live inside wood or fungi. These can also be reared, though it is often not so easy. Whole fungi with the larvae inside can be kept in containers. Pieces of wood or bark known to have larvae can also be kept this way. Larvae in wood or fungi often take a lot longer to develop. One of the main causes of failure is fungal growth on the food stuff. Yes, even fungi will be attacked by other fungi! The best way around this is to keep them well aired.

The larvae of different species have different life cycles. These can usually be looked up in books or on the internet. The main differences to be aware of are at which stage an insect spends the winter. Some over-winter as eggs, some as larvae, some as pupae and others as adults. Species that over-winter as larvae tend to be the most difficult to rear in captivity. These are best found in the spring after hibernation. If you intend to release adult insects it should be at the site where the larvae were found.

Seasons and Weather

What you find on any field trip will be affected by the season and the weather. Bumblebees, for example, can be seen quite early in the year. The hibernating queens come out with the earliest warm days to find places to build nests. Solitary bee species tend to come out later when the average temperature is a little higher. Many wasp species, relatives of the bees, tend to prefer much warmer days. The same principles are true for most insect groups, some like it hot! However, there are insects to be found all year round. Some species will appear as adults in spring only, they will be around for a few weeks then disappear until the following spring. Other species are around during the summer or autumn. However, there are species that appear in spring and then reappear in late summer. Generally speaking, spring and autumn are more productive in terms of adult insects than high summer. During the summer it is usual to find more larval stage insects.

Insect numbers can be severely affected by the weather. The longer the weather remains reasonable, the more insects there will be. If a weather front blows through, especially one with heavy rain and strong winds, insect populations can be decimated. It usually takes 48 hours or so after a weather event for numbers to re-build. Many late season species will survive well into autumn and even part of winter if the weather is mild. They tend to disappear after we have had several successive frosty nights and cold days. Some will re-appear during winter warm spells. Whenever you go on a mini-beast safari take the weather into account.

Even the time of day will determine the species of insects that you will see. Some insects can be active throughout the day. However, many have set routines. Some will start the day early to go foraging before too many predators wake up. Then they will try to find a mate. Others will not stir until the temperature is higher, around mid-day. Many moths along with a number of beetles and insects from other groups are nocturnal. So, if you are looking for specific species you need to have some idea of their daily routine.

Most species of insects have cycles of abundance. This means that each species will have years when it is relatively common and years when they are hard to find. These cycles are driven by long-term weather patterns and the interactions between prey/host species and their predators/parasites. What this means for the entomologist is that species can seem to appear and disappear from one year to the next. This is one reason for the need to collect species data year after year. This is the only way we can find out if a species is at a low point in its cycle or if it has become rare or even extinct at a particular site.

Identification

The most important aspect of amateur entomology is correct identification of your specimens. A specimen without a correct name is just an insect, possibly having died for nothing. As mentioned already, many common and brightly coloured insects can be found in popular insect guidebooks. It is probably best to start with such species as they can be easily verified from your photographs by a county recorder. Most insects, however, cannot be identified so easily.

There are specialised books available for some groups of insects. These can be a bit pricey, so you may want to use other methods first. On social media there are numerous insect related interest groups that you can join. Most of them have experts or experienced amateurs who will help. However, you need to be able to take reasonable close-up photographs. Also, you tend to get credit and more help if you are at least trying to identify specimens for yourself. These groups will allow you to get many insects identified that do not appear in the popular books.

Ultimately, as your interest and experience grow, you will need to obtain 'identification keys' for the insects you are interested in. Such keys are not available for all our insect groups, simply because they have not yet been devised. Many of the keys available are out-of-date but still useful to some extent. Often old keys are available as free downloads. There are also many keys available in other languages. The most up to date books are better but can be expensive. Despite all the help and literature available you will still find insects that you cannot reliably identify. That does not mean they are not worth bothering with. Recorders will often accept records of specimens identified correctly to genus level.

What are identification keys? These are usually sets of statements that you have to compare your specimen against in order to get to a correct identification. You may need to start with family level keys. The beetle family, Coleoptera, for example is made up of a number of subfamilies. These, in turn, can be made up of tribes and ultimately genre. As a beginner you may not know if a specimen is a longhorn-beetle or a soldier-beetle, for example. The family key for beetles will take you to the correct sub-family of beetles. Then you find a key for that group of beetles and key your specimen through to a species name.

The keys usually have a 'dichotomous' form. This means that they are made up from 'couplets', each part of a couplet describes a different feature (or set of features) that your specimen may or may not have. At the end of each part there is a number to take you to the next couplet. It is important to always read both parts of each couplet. Also, check all the features given in the couplet as some species may have features in common. As you work through the couplets you are taken to the name of your specimen.

Here is an example adapted from an old key for the Aphodius genus of dung beetles.

25 Elytra with pale pilosity (hairs), at least in the apical half. 26
- Elytra lacking pilosity. 27

26 Pronotum fringed with long hairs... contaminatus
- Pronotum not fringed with long hairs.. obliteratus

Having keyed a dung beetle specimen from couplet 1 at the beginning of the key, we arrive at couplet 25. There are two options based on the wing cases being hairy or otherwise. The specimen in question has hairs on the elytra, so we go to couplet 26. Then, we have two options based on whether the specimen has long hairs along the edges of the pronotum. It does, so the species is Aphodius contaminatus.

Aphodius contaminatus

The two species in couplet 26 are remarkably similar and can be found together. At a glance, they look the same. Without the key it would be difficult to know which species you had found. When using older keys, you will often find that the name given for your specimen is no longer valid. However, this is not usually a problem as the new name can be looked up on up-to-date checklists. A bigger problem with old keys is that they are often not complete, new species will have been found and described that do not appear in the key. This problem is harder to solve but usually there will be someone in-the-know on the appropriate social media group or a specialist recorder may be able to help.

It is commonplace these days for people to compare insects they have spotted with images on the internet or by using identification apps. This is not the way to identify insects. Far too many of the insect photographs on the internet are incorrectly named, or just not named at all. This is not just the case for difficult species, it is also true for easier ones! Always refer to books, published keys, dedicated websites or experts on social media groups. You can even approach any museum with a natural history department for help and advice or contact your local recorder.

Some keys are more difficult to use than others. It can be easier if you work with one insect family as you will need to become familiar with the features used in their identification. Different families of insects often have different sets of features that are used in identification keys. Flies, for example, are often covered in hairs and thicker bristles which are important in their identification. The wing cases of beetles often have pits and grooves called 'sculpturing' that are used in keys.

All the minute features of an insect's body will have special names that you will need to become familiar with. These are usually explained at the beginning of a good set of keys or can be looked up. Or, again, refer to the dedicated social media groups. You will need, at the very least, a hand lens of x15 or x20 magnification.

This 2.5mm beetle has tiny lines called striae across its elytra. They can be seen clearly using a x20 hand lens. This feature places the specimen in the genus Ptomaphagus. Then, also using the lens, a feature on the front feet, or tarsi, makes it a male Ptomaphagus subvillosus. Many species can be reliably identified by an amateur using keys and a hand lens to examine small external features such as these.

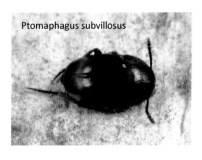
Ptomaphagus subvillosus

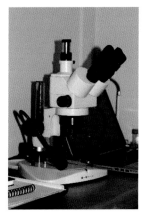

However, there are many more species that require a microscope with x40 or even x80 magnification. These are not cheap. I would not recommend spending that kind of money until you are really sure your interest is going to last.

Microscopes come in a multitude of varieties. A favourite among amateur entomologists is shown opposite. It is a trinocular microscope with a camera port to attach a DSLR type camera which can be plugged into a computer. There is an LED light in the base and a pair of LED flexi-lights for adjustable top lighting.

There are many insects that cannot be identified with certainty from external features. These insects need to be dissected. Do not let this put you off, you do not need to be a scientist with a laboratory. Usually, it is only the genitalia that needs to be dissected out and for most insects this is fairly straightforward. It does, however, mean more kit and more expense! Your personal preferences, level of experience and needs will dictate how far you are prepared to go.

It is important to take note of when and where you find your insect specimens. This includes type of habitat, plant species, time of year and location. All these factors can help with identification. Some species are extremely specific in terms of habitat and plant associations. Others are found at different times of year. A specimen found in April in Sussex, for example, is unlikely to be a late season species known only from the Highlands of Scotland. Identification keys will often give some of these factors, others you will need to look up in books or on the internet. There is a website called NBN Atlas which gives maps of the known distributions of most species. Use it as a guide, it is far from complete.

Does size matter?

The sizes of insects can be measured in a number of different ways. Most commonly, the size of a species is given as the length of the body from the front of the head to the tip of the abdomen, excluding antennae and ovipositors. This measurement will be given as a size range reflecting the individual differences within a species. Some species vary only a little, others vary a lot. Sometimes there is a gender size difference. As an example, the large diving beetle Cybister lateralmarginalis varies from 29mm to 37mm.

Flying insects, such as bees and wasps, are often measured across the wings. Sometimes this measurement is given from wing tip to wing tip with the wings held at right-angles to the body. A better measure is of one forewing from tip to base. This is given as 'forewing length'. Books that give insect sizes will usually state which measurements are being used.

In terms of identification, body length and wing length are mostly irrelevant. At best they can be used to separate related genre where the sizes of species within each genus do not overlap. Only a few species can be separated on size. So, do not become too obsessed with size. As you find and identify a range of species you will become familiar with the expected size ranges of species from different families of insects.

In this book I will give the average sizes of some species just to give some indication of the range of sizes of insects. The size ranges given will be body lengths, wing spans [WS] or forewing lengths [FWL]. Most British insects are quite small, our smallest beetle is just 0.6mm. Do not expect to find giants!

Insect Names

The result of the identification process is a scientific name for your specimen. These names are 'binomial', they have two parts. The first name is the 'genus' to which the insect belongs. A genus is a group of very closely related species. The second name is the 'specific' name. Some species will have a third name, this indicates a 'sub-species'. This binomial system was introduced by the Swedish botanist Carl Linnaeus in the 18th century and has stood the test of time.

People will tell you that the scientific names are difficult and that there are certain ways to pronounce the words. In fact, it is no more difficult than remembering all the names of your family and friends, along with their phone numbers and email addresses. You will learn them as you go along, the more you use them the easier they are to recall. It does not really matter how the words sound as you will mostly be using them in the written form. The important thing is the correct name correctly spelled.

The vast majority of insects do not have common English names. Some common species have had different names in different areas and at different times in history. This is the problem with names in ordinary English. What is a 'tortoiseshell' butterfly to some people is a 'kingy' to others. There are no rules governing who gives these names or which should be used.

Scientific names, on the other hand, often have meaning specific to the species. They cannot be given or changed by popular fashion. There is a process by which names are given and accepted. These names can change but there has to be valid reasons for the change. These changes are then documented and listed in the official checklists of species. These checklists will give the entire history of name changes for any given species. Also, the scientific names of species are accepted and known by entomologists all over the world.

In this book all species will be given by their current scientific names. Where they exist, their accepted common names will be included. There is a movement to introduce common names for all species. This is not universally welcomed and may not work in the long term so do not rely on common names.

Beware the Copycats!

Identifying insects correctly is made more complicated by unrelated species having a similar appearance. It is also the case that closely related species may look completely different. Some species have evolved to be direct mimics. This often happens when a poisonous species is mimicked by an edible species. Predators learn to avoid poisonous insects as they are usually distasteful. So, a non-poisonous species can avoid being eaten by being a good mimic. Other species can be indirect mimics. This can happen through a process called 'convergent evolution'. This occurs when insects living in isolated but similar habitats evolve similar features.

Is that a Wasp?

Not everything with black and yellow stripes is a wasp. Not all wasps have black and yellow stripes.

Clockwise from top left:

Clytus arietis (Wasp Beetle)

Dasysyrphus albostriatus (Hoverfly)

Vespa crabro (Hornet)

Crossocerus tarsatus (Solitary Wasp)

Spot the Ladybird!

Conventional wisdom tells us that ladybirds, Coccinellidae family, are spotty black and red beetles. However, many ladybirds do not conform to this stereotype. There are a number of species which you would not instantly recognise as ladybirds.

Clockwise from top left:
Coccidula rufa
Myzia oblongoguttata (Striped Ladybird)
Anatis ocellata (Eyed Ladybird)
Aphidecta obliterata (Larch Ladybird)

One family, four quite different beetles.

Within any species there is a certain amount of natural variability. Humans are no exception! In some species this variability can be extreme, but it is usually more subtle. This kind of variability can make identification to species level quite difficult.

These are all specimens of the Harlequin Ladybird, Harmonia axyridis. It is an extremely variable species with many forms that often resemble other ladybirds.

A further complication is sexual dimorphism. This simply means that the males and females of a species do not look the same as each other. This can be confusing for a beginner who is unfamiliar with such species.

The wings of the male and female Purple Hairstreak butterflies, Favonius quercus, are different. This is an example of sexual dimorphism.

Many insects take at least a few hours to mature after emerging as adults. This can lead to specimens not looking the same colour as the images you might find in a book. An immature adult insect is known as teneral. This is particularly common in beetles and dragonflies.

These specimens are both Paranchus albipes (a ground beetle). The one on the left is an immature adult, it is a teneral specimen.

Experience with a broad range of insects will soon make sense of all these variations. Do not be put off by these complexities. It is all this variety that makes the insects so fascinating and worth studying.

A much rarer complication is gynandromorphy. If an insect is a gynandromorph then it is half male and half female. Gynandromorphs are rarely seen in the wild. Some Lepidoptera, particularly the blue butterflies, seem to be more prone. However, the only example I have ever encountered was a sawfly.

Strongylogaster multifasciata (a sawfly): In this example the head is female on the left and male on the right. The abdomen is male on the left and female on the right. Wildlife weird at its best!

Recording Insects

The best reason for catching and identifying insects as an amateur entomologist is for recording purposes. This means, when you are certain of the identification of your specimens, you lodge records of your finds with a relevant organisation. This can be one of any number of bodies. Most counties now have organised biological recording systems, these can be found by searching on the internet or simply enquire at your local conservation trust. There are also a number of national recording schemes. Some of these are for specific groups of insects, such as the UK Beetle Recording Scheme. Others are recording schemes for all native wildlife. The scheme called 'BRC iRecord' can be found on the internet. It is a general wildlife recording database with an easy to use interface. You simply input your records and add photographs if you have any. Eventually an expert will look at your records and verify them or otherwise. The records from iRecord are transferred to the NBN Atlas. This is a national database of records and a mapping scheme. It is a useful reference tool for checking distributions of species.

Recording of insect sightings needs to be formal and accurate. It is best if this starts in your own personal recording system. There are some basic requirements without which a record is useless. A record needs to include the name of the specimen, the date it was observed, the location where it was found and the type of habitat. It is best to include a 6-figure grid reference which can be found from the relevant Ordnance Survey Map. Grid references can also be found online. You should also include the name of the recorder (person who found/saw the specimen) and the name of the determiner (the person who identified the specimen) if different. (It may be that you had a specimen identified by an expert on a social media group for example.)

Here is an example of a checklist. This is part of a checklist for British Ichneumons.

Adelognathus acantholydae Kasparyan, 1986
Distribution: Scotland
Notes: NMS, det Shaw, added here

Adelognathus brevicornis Holmgren, 1857
Nomenclature:
Limbatus Thomson, 1888
Montivagator Aubert, 1976
Distribution: England, Scotland, Ireland

Adelognathus brevicornis was named as such by August Holmgren in 1857. This is the currently accepted name for the species. It has had two previous names, these are given under 'Nomenclature'.

The accepted name of a species can change over time for a variety of reasons. Each of the succession of names will have an 'author', the person who gave it that name. It can be useful if you include the author of the name you are using for your specimen. The name of the author will follow the name of the specimen in an official checklist. The more information the better, but it needs to be accurate and honest. Falsified records fool no-one and are completely worthless.

If you are serious and intend to record many different species it is usually best to have some kind of numbering system for your records. In these days of computers, it is fairly easy to build a catalogue of records in a program such as Excel. Each group of insects has an official British checklist. These can usually be found on the internet and are often free to download. They are convenient starting points for a coded recording system. Simply obtain the relevant list and give each species an individual number.

Here is an example from my own filing system. I have a checklist of British Neuroptera (N). To this list I added a code number for each species. My Neuroptera finds are then recorded using a simple spreadsheet format.

Code	Name	Date	Site	Grid	No.	Habitat	Comments
N001.01	Atlantoraphidia maculicollis	04/05/2019	Broc Hill	SJ975200	1 Adult	Wooded heath	beaten from pine
N001.02	Atlantoraphidia maculicollis	04/05/2019					
N001.03	Atlantoraphidia maculicollis	04/05/2019					
N004.01	Xanthostigma xanthostigma	01/06/2019	Chorlton	SJ805375	1 Female	Hedgerow	swept from hedge

The code N001 refers to Atlantoraphidia maculicollis, a snakefly. I found it on 04/05/2019 at grid reference SJ975200 which is Broc Hill on Cannock Chase in Staffordshire. The decimal parts of the codes refer to individual photographs of the specimen.

Snakefly

The advantage of a filing system in spreadsheet format is that it can easily be sent to recorders. This saves a lot of time for yourself and the person collating all the records. My personal preference for submitting records is to contact the local recorder and post them my records, by email, in a slightly adapted version of my own filing system. I find that, if you build a good working relationship with the local recorders, they will be familiar with your methods of identification and can be of assistance in many ways. You will not necessarily find this with some of the national database systems. Each system has its advantages and disadvantages. Try them and see which best suits your needs.

Most books about entomology suggest the use of a notebook in the field. This can be used to note down all the details you need to include in your records. You can also note lots of extra detail, such as the weather and other types of insects, plants and animals seen at the site. All this information is potentially of value. The main disadvantages are time and wet, grubby hands. If you are catching many different species, you may not have time to make too many notes as you go along. A notebook that is covered in mud is not really attractive and your notes may become unreadable. Some people prefer to put labels on their collecting pots and make a few notes on those.

Many entomologists keep journals for recording details of field trips. These can include descriptions of habitat, plant/animal communities present at the site and the weather etc. If you have a particularly good memory you might not want to make notes at all. If you do this, it is important to put as much detail as you can into your filing system later. Remember, though, it needs to be accurate and honest.

Collecting Insects

Collecting insects is usually frowned upon these days, especially outside entomological circles. However, most insects cannot be identified without examining specimens and running them through the relevant keys. Many will need dissection for certain identification. So, the options are catch, identify, release or catch, identify, keep.

If you are going to collect specimens you should do so with a purpose, insects should not be collected for the sake of ornament. The days of collectors proudly displaying their catches are long gone. A collection of specimens, especially of species not often collected, can be quite valuable to science. Such a collection needs to have the specimens correctly labelled with the same details as given in your records. They should also be mounted and preserved in an accepted manner for the species being collected. Your collection needs to be deposited with a museum to be of real use, preferably one with an established natural history department. Sadly, most collections have, in the past, been destroyed when their collectors have died. Any journals relating to your collections should be deposited with them.

There are some perfectly good reasons for a serious amateur entomologist to have a specimen collection. The records you submit are potentially of more value to science if you have a 'voucher' specimen of each species. These can be examined by future researchers and new knowledge can be obtained by doing so. New identification keys, for example, are devised by researchers examining many thousands of museum specimens. This is one reason why the accuracy of identification and other details given with your records and specimens is so important.

There are many groups of insects that are best identified by comparing them with specimens that have already been reliably identified. This is because the features required for identification are necessarily comparative. This will become apparent as you gain more experience with a range of keys. The differences in sculpturing on the surfaces of insects, for example, can be quite subtle and hard to describe. The only reliable way around this is to have a set of specimens to compare with. Some museums will allow you to check your finds against their specimen collections.

It is not necessary to have drawers full of individual species, as past collectors have done. I would not recommend more than ten specimens of a difficult species. These can be collected from one site or from different sites. Each option can give different information about a particular species as long as the recorded details are accurate.

Nor would I recommend collecting common, easy to identify species. Most museum collections will already be overloaded with such species. If you are going to collect, try to build a collection of species that are not often collected, without deliberately targeting rarities. We are not Victorian trophy hunters! The museums will be more likely to accept good collections of species they do not already have. Remember, every museum is just a building, each has its own limited storage capacity so make your collection worth storing. If this really interests you, speak to your local museums and ascertain whether or not they would like a collection of local species and which insect groups they would be more interested in.

In the interests of conservation, if you find a species that you know or suspect to be rare do not be tempted to collect every individual. Insects are not antiques or trophies, they are living creatures with the same right to exist as the collector has. The aim should always be to find, record and enjoy. The aim is not to destroy. Also, some species are legally protected. The Law gives you the responsibility of knowing which!

Mounting and Storing

Insects in collections are usually 'mounted' in some way. The more traditional methods involve putting pins through your specimens. There are not really any set rules, but some methods are more acceptable than others. This is particularly true if you intend to deposit your collection at a museum. It would be a good idea to visit a museum with insect collections to see how it is done. You may even be able to speak to their curator and get some free advice.

Pins come in a variety of types, lengths and thicknesses (gauge). It is now often recommended that we use standard 38mm long stainless-steel pins with heads. The pin should be thick enough to be stable but not so thick as to damage the specimen. The specimen should be about two thirds up the pin. This is to leave room for long dangling legs and for labels.

It has become fashionable now to use carded specimens. Small beetles, for example, can be glued to a piece of stiff card and the pin is then put through the card leaving the insect undamaged. Other insects may be card-pointed. A piece of card with a point is glued to one side of the insect. This leaves most of the identifying features visible and is becoming a popular method for smaller parasitic wasps, for example. These insects have long legs and wings with many identifying features on their thoraxes.

The most important aspect of mounted specimens is the labels. Small pieces of thin card or paper should be used to write on all the relevant data for each specimen. This is most of the basic data used for your records. It should be written in small and neat lettering. You can use two or three labels if necessary. Your mounted specimens should be stored in dry conditions, preferably in air-tight boxes. Storage boxes can be purchased or home-made. You will need to protect your collection from mould and insects that will eat them.

Many smaller insects are not suitable for pinning or carding. These are more usually stored in glass vials of alcohol solution. This is particularly useful for tiny aphids or springtails, for example. A solution of 70% alcohol is often recommended.

If you intend to collect specimens, there are books that will show you the accepted methods for your chosen group of insects. All the equipment you need can be purchased from any number of entomological suppliers. If you are unsure of your needs they will often advise if you tell them what you are collecting.

Photography

It has to be said, I am not the World's best photographer! Then, I do not intend to produce competition winning photographs. I take photographs as a means to record my finds for myself. That said, this book is produced for budding amateurs and it is intended to show what an amateur can do without too much expense. That includes not spending a fortune of photographic kit. So, it is fitting that my amateurish photos are used. Professional looking photographs of tiny insects are a specialist area. They are difficult, time-consuming and expensive to produce. This just adds to the cost of producing books, a cost that is naturally passed on to the consumer!

I used to take photos to identify my finds until I progressed to more difficult species. I now identify most specimens in hand using the relevant keys. The best-looking insect photographs, I think, are taken in the wild using natural light. However, this is rarely practical, most insects do not sit and pose for you! More often than not, you will obtain one photograph and lose the specimen. As most insects cannot be identified without the specimen, you end up with lots of images of 'things'. The alternative is to catch the insects and photograph them later in a more controlled environment.

Insect collectors are familiar with killing jars and killing fluid (Ethyl Acetate). These can be readily purchased from entomological suppliers. With practice, it is possible to use a killing jar to put specimens to sleep if you do not want to kill them. A killing jar can be any glass jar with a metal screw on lid. I use a pad of cotton wool to which a few drops of killing fluid can be added. Place the specimen in the jar until it stops moving. Look for legs twitching, this is a sign that the specimen is not quite ready. The specimen should be subdued long enough for a few photos or to run it through a key. It should recover fairly quickly for release. I now rarely lose any specimens using this method.

The method above allows you to pose specimens so as to take photographs from different angles. You also have more control over light and background. If you just need images as a record or for identification purposes this can be easily achieved. If you want artistic or photographically correct images you can do that too. Though this usually takes more time and better equipment!

Some enthusiasts place insects in a fridge for a short while. This is an alternative to using a killing jar to stun them. It can be effective, but it does tend result in more dead insects. Larger specimens and species that spend the winter as adults are more likely to survive this method.

Many insects are identified by features on their sides or under-sides. These are not normally seen in straightforward snapshots. A typical set of photos for the purpose of identification would need to show all the relevant features as clearly as you can get them. The photos needed will depend on the type of insect. A set of photos for hymenopterans, for example, might include full body, upper thorax, lower thorax and wing veins. The following two images are of a female Apechthis rufata.

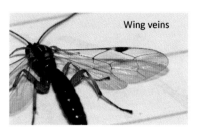

Photography, in general, is more accessible than it has ever been. Most of us now carry mobile phones with built-in cameras. These are often good enough to give photographs of insects that can be identified from snap-shots. If you are more serious, you may want to purchase a DSLR camera and a macro lens for dedicated close-up photography. There are advantages and disadvantages to all types of photographic kit. The choice comes down to needs, cost and personal preference.

The main advantage, for the entomologist, of a DSLR with a macro lens is the quality of the close-up images. This is the most important factor when it comes to identifying specimens from photographs. It is possible to identify more than just large brightly coloured species if your images show fine detail. This is best achieved with the above kit. Even better fine detail photographs can be created by a method known as 'stacking'. This involves taking a large number of shots that are exactly the same except for the focus. These are then 'stacked' using computer software. The best bits are stitched together to make one really sharp photo. It costs more and is rather time consuming. The choice is yours!

When looking at specimen photos anywhere remember that most of the images will not be life-size. A tiny insect of 2mm in length will not make a good picture for a book if shown life-size. Most of the images in this book have been re-sized to standardise them through the book. The actual sizes of some specimens will be given for reference.

Why do entomology?

Many people start doing entomology simply out of curiosity, often as a child fascinated by 'bugs' in the garden. However, the majority will lose interest as their lives change and develop. Of those who remain interested, very few will go far beyond a casual observance. I know of quite a few enthusiasts who at least go as far as recording insects seen in their own gardens. Often such people believe that going any further requires expert knowledge and is too difficult. They also tend to believe that anything they might find would be of little significance. This is far from the truth.

The correct identification and recording of insects are, in fact, no more difficult than most other hobbies and you do not need to be a qualified expert. The work of amateur entomologists is of real value and significance. Extraordinarily little is known about most of our insects. Even basic knowledge such as distribution and population sizes are severely lacking. Every record submitted by every amateur entomologist adds valuable data to our knowledge base.

In Britain we have destroyed almost all our natural habitats. Most of what we see as 'wild' is, in fact, man-made habitat. We have been re-landscaping these islands for thousands of years. Add in chemical pollution, mainly from agriculture, and climate change and the picture may seem rather gloomy. We have precious little wilderness or wildlife left. The majority of species are squeezed into small pockets of suitable habitat. Only the real generalists can prosper in a man-made world.

A more positive view is that we have a large and fascinating range of species for such a small island! We have a fantastic patchwork of habitats. Most of us are within easy reach of woodlands, fields and wetlands of some description. Every macro and micro-habitat hides something different. We know so little about the vast majority of species that we cannot truly define the status of our insect fauna. The flip side of this is that every one of us can go out and find something new to add to our knowledge. That knowledge could be the saviour of our wildlife.

The decline of Britain's birds has been well documented for decades. This has allowed for changes in legislation to protect birds and for conservation groups to target the most endangered species, halting and even reversing their declines. Without the countless 'birders' counting and recording the species they encountered we would not have known how serious the bird declines were and we may have lost many species.

The same cannot be said of British insects. Popular surveys have shown the declines of our butterfly species. Conservation measures are being put into place to help a few of the most endangered. The Large Blue, Phengaris arion, became extinct in Britain and had to be re-introduced. It is the kind of basic knowledge that we as amateur entomologists can provide that allows these declines to be noticed and conservation to take place.

There is a general 'sense' that many of our insects are in decline and potentially in serious trouble. However, there simply is not enough data to show distribution or population trends for most species. Are most of our insects in trouble? We think they might be, but we do not really know. Until there is real evidence, in the form of collected data, not much conservation can take place and there will be no pressure for new legislation to protect our insects. Only a handful out of the 24 000 species are currently protected by law.

This is where we, as amateur entomologists, can help. Every record submitted by every one of us puts a dot on a map. These dots build up a picture that tells us how widespread a species might be. The density of dots can tell us how common a species is at any particular location. Other details will build a picture of preferred habitats and, by inference, the distribution of suitable sites. All this information can lead to effective conservation measures where and when needed. It can also provide the evidence to push for legislation to protect our insects and their habitats. Local Councils, for example, are required to identify Sites of Biological Importance within their boundaries. This information is used to inform Planning Application decisions in order to protect local biodiversity. Much of the data used for such purposes comes from local amateur entomologists submitting records to their local biological records office. These are often run jointly by councils and the Wildlife Trusts.

The presence, or absence, and population sizes of insects can also tell us much more about the quality of habitats and the state of the environment. When species disappear or new ones arrive, this can signal a change in the habitat or eco-system. Heathlands, for example, will often turn into woodlands if not managed correctly. Heathland species will decline, and woodland species will increase. Heathland is a habitat with a priority status. So, careful monitoring of a range of species is needed to keep a check on the quality of the habitat. Genuine ancient woodland is exceedingly rare in Britain. We can tell if a woodland is ancient by the range of insects associated with it. Pollution events often come to light when someone notices the disappearance of water beetles from a local stream or pond. This can lead to polluters being prosecuted and habitats being cleaned and restored.

Many species of insects are on the move because of climate change. Species from southern counties are now turning up in the Midlands. Species from the continent are crossing the Channel and breeding in the southern counties. All these changes are known about and monitored by the collection of data. The effects of species moving north into the territories of other species is unknown. Without the collection of distribution and population data we can only guess.

There is precious little funding in Britain for entomological study. Most of the funding available is associated with agriculture and crop pests. So, it is up to the ranks of amateur entomologists to collect large quantities of good quality data. As long as your data is accurate you will find that recorders are happy to take as many records as you have. Every single record is of value. Masses of records could, ultimately, save our wildlife.

There are other more personal benefits from active amateur entomology. Getting out and about in the fresh air is good for the physical and mental wellbeing of all of us. This is true whether you are ten or one hundred and ten. The process of identifying insects and compiling records is a good mental exercise. This can be of benefit to school children as part their educational development. It could also help older people maintain the effectiveness of their faculties. Joining local groups of like-minded people can be good for childhood development or as a means of combatting loneliness in older age. Each and every one of us can take something from the hobby. Personally, I do it for the sheer pleasure of being outdoors and keeping my inquisitive brain active.

Can you help insects in other ways? Most conservation organisations, as well as needing to raise funds, have an army of volunteers. In most cases these armies are nowhere near big enough. Conservation volunteers donate their time and skills in the cause of all wildlife. This can be in administration, collating records for example, or practical work on nature reserves.

Anyone with time on their hands can offer something. I currently volunteer with Natural England. We work in small groups at one of the best kept secrets in the Midlands! It does not have public access, so volunteering is a way of visiting the site and doing some practical conservation work. I get to work in a fascinating place, to see some good wildlife and meet some interesting people. Win, win, win!

Safety, Respect and the Law

There are many potential dangers out in the countryside. It is easy to get distracted and fall from a height or into a deep pond, for example. Your safety is your responsibility. You should be aware of any hazards at any site you visit before you go. Use the internet, look at the relevant Ordnance Survey maps or simply ask the owner of the site you are planning to visit. Different types of terrain have different hazards. Whatever else you do on a safari, always keep safe. Let someone know where you are going and approximately what time you expect to return. Leave your mobile phone number but be aware that in remote areas you may not get a signal!

If you scoff at the potential dangers, take a look at the hole in this picture. I had the misfortune to fall into this hole. It was covered by rotten chipboard and leaf litter so could not be seen. I just about managed to haul myself out with torn muscles in several places. Off the beaten track with no-one around this could have been a lot more serious!

Most of the land in Britain is in private ownership. There are many miles of public rights of way giving access to much of this land. If you want to access areas off these rights of way, then you should seek permission from the landowners. Be polite and present yourself well and, usually, access will be granted. Always explain why you want to access their land and respect any conditions they might impose. Respect the land, crops and livestock and always close any gates behind you. If you take a dog, keep it on a lead when near livestock. Do not cause damage and do not leave litter or other rubbish behind. You should at least offer a report of your findings to the landowner.

These principles also apply to land owned by conservation groups or by local authorities. The latter are responsible for most town parks and public open spaces. They also often own small local nature reserves and larger country parks. Even though these lands are open to the public you should still speak to the appropriate council official about your activities. Your local Biological/Ecological Recorder should be able to help you with this.

The Wildlife Trusts spend many years of hard work raising money to buy land for conservation. They then continue to raise money and volunteers to manage their reserves. Many of these reserves are open to the public. However, you should always ask for permission to go insect hunting on nature reserves. State your intentions and offer a report of your findings and permission will usually be granted. They will expect you to respect the wildlife, the reserve and other visitors. They will not be happy if you go to their reserves to take away specimens of rare species for your personal trophy collection. You could, at the very least, donate to the Trust. Or, if you have time, you could do some volunteer conservation work. This will go a long way in establishing a good relationship with the Trust and possibly gain you access to reserves that are usually closed to the public.

Natural England (NE) is a government body set up to protect some of our best sites of natural interest. A number of them will be mentioned in this book. These include places important for their geology as well as places of significant wildlife interest. Some of these National Nature Reserves (NNRs) are owned by NE, others are leased from their owners. Many are only accessible by prior permission from the appropriate local NE managers. They are usually amenable to bona fide entomologists, even us amateurs. The same principles apply as for Wildlife Trust reserves. Build up a good rapport with the local NE management and do a bit of volunteering. They will be very grateful as volunteers can be hard to come by and government funding is tight.

This is Chartley Moss NNR. It can only be accessed by permission from the local NE manager. There are no public rights of way through the reserve. It is fascinating geologically and has an impressive invertebrate fauna. The surface you see is 3m of peat formed by sphagnum mosses. Under the peat is a lake 10m deep! The pine trees in the image have drowned because their roots are sitting in acidic water!

It is your responsibility to know how the law affects your activities. Very few British insects are directly protected by the law. However, habitats, vegetation and other animals that might be affected by your insect hunting may be protected. You might, for example, disturb nesting birds in the spring or find amphibians hibernating in rotten logs during the winter. Experience will help you develop good field craft, this will reduce the disturbance your activities create.

Good field craft should include a respect for all wildlife and habitats. Do not kill or cause the demise of species you are not recording, including other invertebrates, vegetation or other animals. Be mindful of habitat damage.

Some micro-habitats, in particular, are easily destroyed completely. When looking for insects under bark, for example, do not be tempted to strip entire trees. It is only necessary to peel back small areas of bark, leave the rest for the insects to live in and thrive. If a tile falls off your roof it is not the end of the world. However, if the roof is completely blown off by a storm it could be life changing!

Our insect fauna needs thousands of amateur entomologists to go out and find, identify and record. The more data we collect, the greater the prospects of our insects surviving and thriving for future generations to study and enjoy. This will not work if we have thousands of people trampling and destroying everything in order to fill personal tick lists. Enjoy your pursuits, make your data available, respect the wildlife and leave enough for future enthusiasts to follow in your footsteps.

Part Two: Mini-beast Safaris

Most of us have seen adverts for expensive safari holidays on big game ranches in Africa. The beauty of mini-beast safaris is that every square meter of land is a big game ranch in miniature, even in your back yard. Everything is a lot smaller, but all the same drama is there and more besides. Mini-beast safaris have herds of grazers being stalked by vicious predators. There are also more alien dramas, such as parasitic wasp grubs living inside caterpillars until they burst through the skin to pupate. Best of all, it is largely free to watch and you do not have the hassle of customs and waiting around in airport lounges!

Garden and Park Safaris

Gardens and parks constitute one of our largest, most readily available habitats. In built up areas they can be the only habitat within easy reach. Every garden in a street can be different, each with its own range of plants and insects. The wildlife in a town park will depend on its age, history and management.

Take a close look at the average suburban garden. What do you see? There will be lawns (grasses), shrubs (hedges) and a scattering of trees. In places there might be an undeveloped corner with a cluster of trees (copse). There will also be sheds, ponds, compost heaps and pets that poo! In fact, the suburbs have most of the habitats you will find in the average piece of farmland.

Even the blandest looking garden and most over-manicured park will have a range of insects for you to find and identify. The best advantage of a garden, of course, is privacy. If you start your insect forays in a garden, you will have time to try different techniques with a variety of equipment. Then, when you venture beyond the garden gate, you will be more confident and less conscientious about people watching!

The greatest diversity will be found in old gardens and parks with mature trees, overgrown shrubs and neglected areas. Old graveyards too can be particularly good places for insects. It is important that a good percentage of the plant life is native, or at least derived from native species.

Our garden has a mature oak that is rotting inside the trunk. We have hedges of hawthorn with some Blackthorn, conifers, Ivy and a few fruit trees. There is a wildflower bed that we planted a couple of years ago. We do not trim the hedges too often so that moth and other larvae can survive long enough to become adults.

Look for micro-habitats within your garden. In particular, look for piles of dead wood or brick and rubble. These will provide places for many species to hide in. You can always create these habitats yourself. Piles of rotting grass cuttings and hedge clippings left undisturbed will soon attract a whole community of invertebrates.

Rubble piles will attract ground beetles and springtails.

Piles of hedge/grass cuttings will attract a variety of species.

A pitfall trap will catch anything crawling across the ground.

Each tree and shrub species in your garden should be searched separately. Use a beating tray on the hedges and trees, or use a sheet placed on the ground. Try not to damage the trees though! If you grab hold of some branches and give them a good shake this will avoid the damage that can be caused by a beating stick. This is not recommended for thorny shrubs, though. At least, not without gardening gloves!

On sunny days flower beds will be full of bees, bugs and beetles. Try using your sweep net around the lawn, borders and flower beds. Sweep the air too, especially above the borders and lawns on warm still days. Using a suction sampler on lawns and under hedges will reveal the presence of a number of ground beetles, ground bugs and possibly other insects. Mature compost heaps or leaf litter from under trees and shrubs can be sieved for specimens. Look out for spiders and tiny predatory pseudoscorpions, these will be feeding on small insects such as springtails.

NB: Too much sweeping can be damaging to flowers. As an alternative method, try shaking tall flowers over a beating tray. This method is particularly good for stiff plants such as woody herbs and shrubby species. It can reveal species missed by a sweep net.

Do not forget to check around your pond if you have one. Even the smallest garden pond will attract insects. Also, look in outbuildings and your house for insects and other invertebrates. Holes in walls, like this one, can be home to mason or leafcutter bees and other insects. Watch for them hovering about by your house or garden walls. On sunny days south facing walls can get quite warm, even in winter. This warmth will attract insects all year round.

The principles for searching in gardens and parks are the same. Many older parks were planted with Sycamore and limes. Sycamore does not have a great diversity of associated species as it is not native, but there will still be a number of species on the foliage. The flaky bark of Sycamore is more interesting. Many insects will hibernate under large flakes of bark, to find them requires removing a few flakes. This does not usually harm the tree, but you should still be careful and do not remove too much. You will find most species present after removing two or three decent size flakes. There will usually be spiders too, I have found five different species on one Sycamore tree.

This Sycamore stump shows the typically flaky bark of these trees. It also indicates that there are likely to be species associated with dead and rotting wood in this particular park. This stump is a micro-habitat worthy of some attention. The gaps between root buttresses around a stump like this will provide hiding places for many invertebrates. The stump may be home to bark beetles or other wood-boring species. Check for fungi and their associated insects too.

Lime tree species have a much greater range of associated insects. They are always worth spending some time on. As usual, check the foliage with a net or beating tray. Check the leaves for signs of insects such as galls and feeding damage.

Lime trees usually develop a thick bush of twig-like branches around the base of the trunk. This bush accumulates leaf litter and other debris from the tree and makes a hiding place for all sorts of invertebrates. Insects will hibernate here, and some moth larvae will crawl down the tree and pupate in the leaf litter.

Insects can leave all sorts of signs that betray their presence. Galls have already been mentioned. The larvae of many insects are so small that they actually live inside leaves. They feed between the upper and lower surfaces of the leaves, this results in a 'leaf-mine'. Once you know what they are, leaf-mines become pretty obvious. Many are created by small moth species, such as the one on the left. Others are created by sawfly larvae, such as the one on the right.

These two mines were found on Silver Birch, another tree commonly planted in parks. It is a bit more specialist, but many insects can be identified from the mines they leave behind. Some are actually easier to identify this way.

Some parks may have wild corners. This one has a disused railway line. It is overgrown and wild. Such places are reservoirs for all sorts of wildlife. However, you should check whether or not they are accessible. They may be out of bounds to the public on safety grounds.

Most parks will have a pond and flower beds. However, the flower beds are paid for with public money and it will not be appreciated if you go knocking off all the flower heads with a sweep net. The ponds are likely to have fish in them, probably ornamental carp, so you may not be allowed to do any pond dipping.

Remember to ask permission before doing insect searches in public spaces. Contact the local parks department for permission to survey parks. Ask at the vicarage before searching in graveyards. These areas are important to people for other reasons and need to be respected. Much of what entomologists do, hanging around in the bushes etc, can look strange to other people. You need to cover yourself by having permission, preferably in writing. Then, if anyone should ask, you can show that what you are doing is legitimate and legal!

What follows is a collection of invertebrates found in our garden or other urban habitats such as parks and waste ground. Any of these species can be found and identified by a keen amateur. This section will also introduce you to some of the insects orders and families. Remember that many common species are not restricted to particular macro-habitats.

64

All butterflies and moths are in the order Lepidoptera. Some of our most well-known insects are butterflies. We have less than sixty species, several of them will turn up in gardens or local public spaces. It was a surprise, though, when the Orange-tip butterfly, Anthocharis cardamines, [46mm WS] bred in our wildflower patch.

The male is easy to identify as it is our only species with orange wing tips. Both sexes have a chequered green underside. The female, though, can be mistaken for the Small White, Pieris rapae, as she does not have the orange flashes. The larvae can be reared easily in captivity. Its distinctively shaped pupa would not be easy to find in the wild.

The Holly Blue, Celastrina argiolus, [30mm WS] is the most likely blue butterfly to be seen in gardens or parks. It is unusual in that it has two generations a year with each generation feeding on a different plant. The larvae of one generation use Ivy and the other use Holly. These two plants can often be found growing together in old gardens, parks and cemeteries.

Many of our insects evolved to live in wooded habitats, including the Red Admiral, Vanessa atalanta [70mm WS]. They have adapted to man-made environments and can be seen commonly in urban areas. They are particularly fond of feeding on Buddleia flowers planted in gardens and parks.

The sub-family to which the Red Admiral belongs is sometimes called the brush-footed butterflies. They only have two pairs of legs, instead of the usual three pairs. The front pair is reduced and has a brush-like appearance and it is not used for walking.

Several members of the sub-family use Common Nettle as the larval foodplant, including the Red Admiral (above) and the Small Tortoiseshell, Aglais urticae, [55mm WS] (left and below). The larvae can often be found living gregariously (together) in large numbers. The early instars construct a communal web of silk for protection.

When the larvae are nearly full-grown they will spread out and look for somewhere to pupate. This is usually on a nearby plant stem. This association with nettle beds makes them easy to find in urban areas around parks and waste ground. The larvae are very easy to rear in captivity.

Adult butterflies can be caught in flight with a butterfly net or swept from flowers and other vegetation. Be aware that butterfly wings are delicate, a wet net will ruin them. In times past it was commonplace to have large collections of butterfly specimens. Today, this is frowned upon and is completely unnecessary. Many of our butterflies are in serious trouble. Since they can usually be identified from photographs it is best to leave them alone. It will be necessary to photograph the underside of some species, but this can usually be done in the wild.

Traditionally, butterflies and moths were thought to be different and distinct and were treated separately. We now understand that there is no clear distinguishing feature to separate them and we treat them all as Lepidoptera. Likewise, there is a traditional but artificial separation of moths into 'macro-moths' and 'micro-moths'. Most larger moths are classed as macro and the smaller moths as micro.

The vast majority of moths are nocturnal, though you can disturb them from their hiding places during the day. The Silver Y, Autographa gamma, [37mm WS] is active day and night. It is an immigrant commonly seen in gardens.

The Tineidae family contains many species that live around humans. This one is a Tinea pellionella [13mm WS] found in our house. Commonly known as clothes moths, their larvae live in tube-shaped cases made of silk.

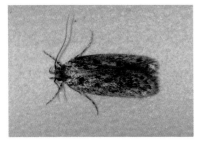

House-moths belong to the Oecophoridae. The Brown House-moth, Hoffmannophila pseudospretella, [22mm WS] will live on any organic matter, including the pages of your favourite insect books!

Many moth larvae can be found on trees and hedges in urban areas. The Lime Hawkmoth, Mimas tiliae, lays eggs on lime trees and is commonly found in town parks.

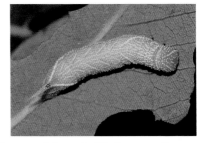

This micro-moth larva is Ditula angustiorana. We found numbers of these on our hawthorn hedges. They do not cause any significant damage.

Some of the most commonly observed flies are the colourful hoverflies. They belong to the family Syrphidae. This one, Episyrphus balteatus, [8mm FWL] is often called the Marmalade-fly and is commonly seen in parks and gardens.

Most flies, including hoverflies, do not have common names. This Eristalis tenax [11mm FWL] is also common in urban habitats. There are several similar looking species in the same genus.

This one is Eupeodes luniger [8mm FWL]. Again, there are a number of similar species. Good views of the patterns, the legs and the faces can be helpful in identifying most black and yellow hoverflies.

Many hoverflies can be difficult to place in the correct genus. Not this one though. This is Rhingia campestris [8mm FWL] with its distinctively elongated face.

Volucella inanis [13mm FWL] is a species that has spread dramatically across most of England in recent years, possibly due to climate change. Its larvae live in the nests of wasps, eating their grubs, and the adults will often venture into buildings including houses.

There are many small black hoverflies which often go unnoticed. Most hoverflies should be netted and examined to determine correct identification.

68

Houseflies belong to the family Muscidae. They are not all plain black, this Musca autumnalis [6mm FWL] has orange flanks. Try netting a few and see how many different species you have in and around your house.

Blowflies belong to the family Calliphoridae. Some, like this Calliphora vomitoria [11mm FWL] are often found around human habitation. They are the familiar bluebottles.

Soldierflies, such as this Chloromyia formosa [9mm FWL] often have metallic bodies. They belong to the family Stratiomyidae. Soldierflies enjoy warm sunny weather when adults can be swept from foliage.

This one is Microchrysa polita [5mm FWL]. It can be found on the foliage of hedges basking in sunshine. The larvae of most soldierflies are aquatic. Some may even be found in your garden pond.

This large and colourful fly is Tachina fera [14mm FWL]. It belongs to the family Tachinidae. A number of species from the Tachindae can be found in gardens and parks, though not all are brightly coloured and so easy to identify.

The fly family Cecidomyiidae contains many gall-causing species. This one is Dasineura tympani found on Sycamore leaves. The fly grubs live inside the layers of the leaves creating these obvious blotches. There are other invertebrates that cause galls on Sycamore trees found in parks.

Craneflies belong to the Tipulidae family. Many are familiar to us as daddy-long-legs. This one is Nephrotoma quadrifaria [18mm FWL]. It was found in our garden along with several other species.

This one is Tipula rufina [20mm FWL]. Craneflies can be found all year, but some of our commonest species emerge in autumn. Not all of them are big with long legs. Most of the smaller species tend not to be noticed and often go unrecorded.

This one is Tipula staegeri. Cranefly larvae are mostly associated with damp, rotting organic matter. Some of our most common species live in the soil and are known as 'leatherjackets'. Flocks of birds such as starlings can often be seen pulling leatherjackets out of lawns and greens in parks.

Craneflies have nocturnal habits and will come to any kind of light. They will often come through open windows or doors and bumble about in our houses. They are probably the clumsiest fliers among the flies. Be careful when handling them as the legs are easily broken off.

70

This Chironomus plumosus [6mm FWL] belongs to the Chironomidae fly family. They are familiar insects, some species being common in almost any habitat. Most Chironomids must be caught and examined for certain identification.

This one is Chironomus dorsalis. People usually mistake Chironomid flies for mosquitoes. However, they are non-biting midges. We do have a few mosquito species, but most are encountered less often.

Grasshoppers and crickets belong to the Orthoptera. Crickets can often be found in urban habitats. This one is a female Oak Bush-cricket, Meconema thalassinum [15mm]. Females can be seen laying eggs (ovipositing) in the bark of trees at night. Note the long ovipositor or egg-laying tube.

This one is the Speckled Bush-cricket, Leptophyes punctatissima [15mm]. The male is on the left above. The female is on the right above. The shape of the ovipositor can be used in identifying crickets. The nymph of this species is shown to the right. It looks similar to an adult.

Most beetles, order Coleoptera, in gardens and parks tend to go unnoticed. There are, however, many species associated with urban habitats. There are numerous species living on the ground, often associated with dark damp places, such as under rubble or logs. Some can be found under carpets, especially in doorways.

Ground beetles are in the family Carabidae. The Violet Ground Beetle, Carabus violaceus, [25mm] is common and often found under logs and stones. Be aware, though, not all beetles found on the ground are ground beetles! Also, some ground beetles will climb vegetation.

Many ground beetles are active at night. This Leistus fulvibarbis [7mm] was found in our garden by torchlight. If you have a good population of predatory ground beetles then there must be lots of prey species for them to eat.

This Patrobus atrorufus [8mm] was also found by torchlight in our garden. Remember, you can set pitfall traps to catch beetles living on the ground.

Several species, such as this Poecilus cupreus [12mm] are commonly found on lawns, especially if they are a bit overgrown.

This Agonum mulleri [8mm] was found in our lawn. Many ground beetles have subtle metallic colouring, but most are black.

This Nebria brevicollis [13mm] was found under a log in a park. It is common and can be found in most habitats throughout Britain.

Ocys harpaloides [4.7mm] is often found in leaf litter in many habitats. It spends the winter in tussocks and under bark.

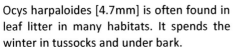

Bembidion is a large genus of small ground beetles. This Bembidion lampros [3.5mm] was found in our garden by suction sampler.

Some Bembidions have orange markings. This Bembidion quadrimaculatum [3.2mm] was also found by suction sampler in the garden.

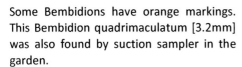

There are 8 species in the genus Calathus. This Calathus melanocephalus [7.4mm] was found by sieving rotting leaf litter in a park

This Anchomenas dorsalis [7mm] was found in leaf litter under the garden hedge by suction sampler. It can be found in many habitats.

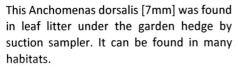

73

Beetles from many families can be found in rotting organic matter. This can be compost heaps, grass cuttings or leaf mould at the edges of ponds. Often these species will be quite small. They can be found by hand searching or sieving.

Cercyon ustulatus [3mm] can be found in the wet litter at the edges of ponds, even in parks. It is not common but can be found across the UK. It is a Hydrophilid species.

This Cercyon unipunctatus [2.9mm] can be found in garden compost heaps. The term for species found around human habitation is 'synanthropic'.

Cryptopleurum minutum [2mm] can be hard to spot in piles of grass cuttings. There are a number of other species in the Hydrophilidae family, mainly living in damp or wet conditions.

Beetles of the Histeridae can also be found in rotting vegetation. This Atholus duodecimstriatus [4.8mm] was sieved from rotting grass cuttings.

Some species of the Leiodidae family are associated with litter and rot habitats. This Catops fuliginosus [3.8mm] was found on a fungus affecting a tree stump in a park.

74

The Monotomidae are often known as root-eating beetles. This Monotoma picipes [2.2mm] was sieved from a compost heap.

There are 44 species of Atomaria in the family Cryptophagidae. They are all very small and mostly hard to identify. This one is Atomaria lewisi [1.7mm].

This one is Atomaria testacea [1.5mm]. Both species were sieved from grass cuttings. Many Atomaria species go unrecorded due to the difficulty in identifying them.

The Latridiidae are all associated with fungoid habitats. This rare Enicmus fungicola [1.8mm] was in a pile of rotting hedge clippings.

This is Alphitobius diaperinus [6.3mm] from the Tenebrionidae. It can be found in stored food but this one was sieved from rotting grass cuttings.

Omonadus floralis [3.1mm] is from the Anthicidae or ant-like flower beetles. They can be quite numerous in grass cuttings and old hay bales.

Date 1/4/24   No   29

Received from Keith Pettyson

The sum of Ten Pounds

For Mini-beast flein's book

With Thanks   Pro-oo

Around one quarter of British beetle species belong to the Staphylinidae family. Many of them can be found in synanthropic habitats. Members of this family are often referred to as 'rove beetles'.

There are quite a few large black rove beetles. They need to be examined for correct identification. This one is Tasgius ater [17mm]. It was found killing woodlice in our bathroom.

Rugilus orbiculatus [4.5mm] is one of several similar species that live in rotting vegetation. We sieved lots of these from our grass cuttings.

Many rove beetles are teardrop shaped like this Sepedophilus littoreus. It was found in hedge clippings that had been left for several weeks.

It is often useful to have a size guide in a photo. Here a plastic ruler is used. This common Tachyporus obtusus [4mm] was sieved from leaf litter in a park.

Anthobium unicolor [3.3mm] is common in leaf litter, moss or, like this one, in fungi. Rove beetles can be found everywhere, in all habitats. Very few can be identified from simple photographs. There is a growing range of keys available.

Beetles from many other families can be found around human habitation. They often survive in remnants of wild habitat or in habitats created by us.

Lesser Stag Beetles, Dorcas parallelipipedus, [26mm] have large wood boring grubs. They require a good supply of large mature trees. This one was found in a rotten Beech trunk in a park. It belongs to the Scarabaeidae family.

Some click beetles, Elateridae, like this pair of Athous haemorrhoidalis, [13mm] can be common in urban habitats.

This Oedostethus quadripustulatus [3.4mm] is usually associated with flood plain meadows. This one, though, was sieved from old garden waste. It always pays to have a look, you never know what will turn up.

Soldier beetles are in the Cantharidae. This one is the common Rhagonycha fulva [8.5mm]. They can often be seen in large numbers, especially on umbellifers, during the summer.

One of a pair of almost identical beetles, Byturus tomentosus [3.6mm] can be really common wherever there are brambles. They can be swept from brambles or other flowers nearby on sunny days.

A number of the beetles found around our homes are considered to be pest species. Some attack stored foods, while others attack furniture or our cherished garden plants.

Tenebrio molitor [15mm] is one of a number of species in the Tenebrionidae family that infest stored foods such as flour. Some, like this one, are also attracted to lights.

Carpet beetles, such as this Anthrenus verbasci, [1.9mm] are in the family Dermestidae. They infest dried animal and plant materials in our homes. Their larvae can infest woollen carpets and clothes.

The family Ptinidae includes many wood boring beetles. Species such as this Anobium punctatum [4mm] are synanthropic. Their larvae tunnel through wooden furniture leaving behind small exit holes and piles of wood dust.

Ochina ptinoides [3.1mm] is also in the Ptinidae. It attacks dead branches of Ivy. Look for them where old Ivy grows up trees or on walls in parks and mature gardens.

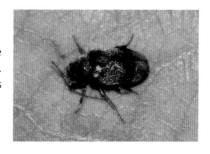

The Lily Beetle, Lilioceris lilii, [7mm] attacks lilies in gardens, leaving characteristic feeding damage on the foliage. It is in the Chrysomelidae family.

Some of our ladybirds are familiar to most people. They belong to the Coccinellidae.

This 7-spot Ladybird, Coccinella septempunctata, [6.5mm] has been parasitised. Underneath it is the cocoon of Dinocampus coccinellae, a parasitic wasp.

Ladybird pupae are usually overlooked. Once you know what they are, it is easy to spot them. This one is the 7-spot.

Ladybird larvae are often colourful too. This one is the 14-spot Ladybird, Propylea quattuordecimpunctata [4mm]. Ladybirds and their larvae can be found on foliage where there are lots of aphids.

Not all ladybirds are red with black spots. This black and yellow 16-spot Ladybird, Tytthaspis sedecimpunctata, [2.7mm] can often be swept from herbage in urban areas.

Weevils belong to several beetle families. Many are pests on garden plants. This Tatianaerhynchites aequatus, [3.6mm] however, can be found on hawthorns including garden hedges. It belongs to the Rhynchitidae family.

Longhorn beetles belong to the family Cerambycidae. They are popular among insect enthusiasts. The name comes from the long antennae possessed by most species. Many have specific requirements, but some can be found in gardens and parks.

Grammoptera ruficornis [5mm] is commonly seen at hawthorn flowers. Longhorns like these can be mistaken for soldier beetles.

This Poecilium alni [6mm] was a surprise find, swept from our wildflower bed. It is found around oaks and Alder.

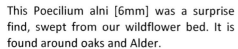

Pogoncherus hispidus [5.5mm] is associated with broad-leaved trees and shrubs. It can be found by beating lime trees in parks.

The scarce Tetrops praeustus [4.5mm] is also associated with broad-leaved trees. I have beaten them from limes and Sycamores in old parks.

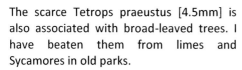

The Chrysomelidae family, or leaf beetles, is a large family with species found wherever there is foliage. This Cryptocephalus pusillus [2.9mm] is one of many associated with trees. It can be found particularly on birches, even in parks. Other species can be swept from flower beds.

The order Hymenoptera contains all our bees, wasps, ants and sawflies. It is a very large and diverse order. There are around 275 species classed as bees in Britain. Some are familiar as pollinators, but others are predators, even attacking bees. Most bee species have specific needs and not many of them can be found in gardens and a lot of them have distinctly southern distributions.

Davies' Colletes, Colletes daviesanus, [6mm FWL] can be found in flowery habitats including gardens. Notice the 'wasp waist' between the thorax and abdomen. All bees have this feature.

The Orange-tailed Mining Bee, Andrena haemorrhoa, [9mm FWL] will visit flowers on shrubs as well as herbage. It can be common in urban areas and will visit gardens. Mining bees usually dig nesting holes in the ground.

The Yellow-legged Mining Bee, Andrena flavipes, [8mm FWL] can also be seen commonly in gardens. Its distribution, though, is more restricted than the previous species being found mainly in the southern half of England.

The Patchwork Leafcutter Bee, Megachile centuncularis, [8mm FWL] cuts off small sections of leaves to construct a nesting cell. This is often in small holes in the outside walls of houses. Look for semi-circular pieces cut from the foliage of shrubs.

Gooden's Nomad Bee, Nomada goodeniana, [8mm FWL] can be seen in gardens. Nomad bees are 'cleptoparasites'. The egg is laid in the nest of another bee, often an Andrena species. The grub destroys the egg or grub of the host and then feeds on its food stores.

The Flavous Nomad Bee, Nomada flava, [9mm FWL] can be found in urban areas. It is often seen in parks and public green spaces. Most Nomada bees resemble stripy wasps.

Bumblebees are familiar to most people, they can be seen in gardens and parks from the end of winter. This one is Bombus pascuorum, the Common Carder Bee [11mm FWL]. It usually nests above ground in grass tussocks, for example.

The Honeybee, Apis melifera, [11mm FWL] is a familiar sight in most gardens. The honeycomb (above) was found on the ground after the tree it was in fell during a storm. The swarm (right) was seen nearby. It was possibly their nest that had been destroyed when the tree fell.

The large black and yellow wasps we are familiar with are social insects. They have queens and build nests, just like many of the bees. However, far more wasp species are solitary, many of them being small black insects that go largely unnoticed.

The Norwegian Wasp, Dolichovespula norwegica, [15mm FWL] is one of our common social wasps. They can often be seen on fence posts and benches chewing off bits of wood. They use it to make paper pulp to build their nests.

The Hornet, Vespa crabro, [25mm FWL] is our largest social wasp. It also builds a paper nest. This one was at head height on the side of split tree trunk. Hornets are not aggressive.

Sapyga quinquepunctata [11mm] is unusually coloured for a wasp. This one was netted from our garden hedge.

Some of the many small black wasps can be found in gardens and parks. This one is Crossocerus megacephalus [8mm].

This Pemphredon lugubris [10mm] was swept from our hedges. Wasps like these tend to be overlooked. However, they can be identified to species with available keys and a x20 hand lens.

The largest group of parasitic wasps is the Ichneumonidae. Most species have long antennae with at least 16 segments, usually many more. Some are internal parasites, eating the host from inside while it is still alive. Others are external parasites and can be seen as grubs on their hosts. The details of the parasitic lifestyles are very varied and for many species the hosts are currently unknown.

Most parasitic wasp species are under recorded, yet they can be found in good numbers everywhere. This Diplazon laetatorius [6mm] is one of many found in our garden.

This Hepiopelmus melanogaster [14mm] was caught in flight over our garden lawn. It is one of several large black species.

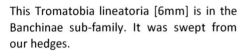

This is a male Ichneumon sarcitorius [10mm]. Unlike most males in the Ichneumon genus this one is easy to identify. Females of this genus are usually easier to identify than males.

This Tromatobia lineatoria [6mm] is in the Banchinae sub-family. It was swept from our hedges.

This Pimpla rufipes [10mm] is a common member of the Pimplinae sub-family. Several were swept from our wildflower bed.

84

Some parasitic wasps pupate in cocoons like many moths species. This cocoon was found by sweeping Ivy in our hedges. It is possibly a species in the genus Cassinaria.

Another large group of parasitic species belongs to the Braconidae family. This Aleiodes similis was swept from our hedges.

Unlike the rest of the Hymenoptera, sawflies do not have the typical wasp-waist. Most species have vegetarian larvae resembling caterpillars. Many sawflies live on only one species of plant making them relatively easy to find. This also helps to identify them. A good number of species can be found in urban areas.

This common Empria tridens [6mm] lives on bramble leaves. It was caught in flight in our garden.

This one is Euura poecilonota [7mm]. It is one several similarly coloured species that need to be caught and examined for correct identification.

This Dolerus haematodes [10mm] is one of many species that feed on grasses. Wherever grasses grow you can find sawflies that live on them.

Bugs belong to the Hemiptera order with around 1830 species in 63 families. The Hawthorn Shieldbug, Acanthosoma haemorrhoidale, [14mm] can be found wherever there is Common Hawthorn.

Bugs have nymphs that usually resemble the adults. This Hawthorn Shieldbug nymph was beaten from our hedgrerow.

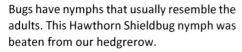

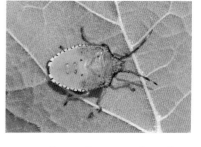

The Parent Bug, Elasmucha grisea, [8mm] can be found on birches, even in parks and gardens. The female sits over her eggs to protect them until they hatch.

The Green Shieldbug, Palomena prasina, [13mm] is in the Pentatomidae family. It is one of the most commonly seen shieldbugs in gadens.

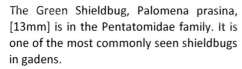

The Dock Bug, Coreus marginatus, [14mm] is in the Coreidae family. It is common and associated with docks in almost any habitat type.

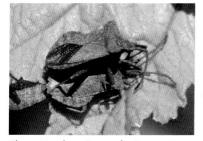

The Nettle Ground Bug, Heterogaster urticae, [6.5mm] is in the Lygaeidae family. It can be seen in large numbers in nettle beds and will hibernate in houses.

Physatocheila dumetorum [2.8mm] is in the Tingidae family, commonly known as lacebugs. This species can be found by beating old lichen covered hawthorns.

Daraeocoris ruber [7mm] is one of around 200 species in the Miridae family. It can be seen almost anywhere feeding on aphids.

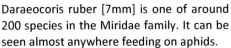

The Ciccadellidae family has around 285 species including the Rhododendron Leafhopper, Graphocephala fennahi [9mm].

The Aphididae family contains around 630 species of aphids. Drepanosiphum platanoidis [3.5mm] can be found on Sycamores in parks.

Many aphid species are pests on cultivated crops and garden plants. Metopolophium dirhodum [2.2mm] is a pest on garden roses.

This Ovatus insistus was beaten from garden hawthorn. Aphids are food for other insects, they attract lots of predators wherever they are. Many aphids avoid being eaten by blending in with the foliage they sit on.

Lacewings belong to the order Neuroptera. There are 66 species in Britain. Many are common and widespread. They all need to be caught and examined. Features of the wing veins are particularly important. This one is a waxfly species, Conwentzia psociformis, it was found on Holly in our garden. The Neuroptera are related to snakeflies (Rhaphidoptera, 4 species), alderflies (Megaloptera, 3 species) and scorpionflies (Mecoptera, 4 species).

There are around 250 Collembola, commonly known as springtails on account of many species being able to jump. Our largest is around 6mm but most are much smaller, many only around 0.5mm. This one is Seira domestica, [3mm] it can be found in houses. Springtails are not easy to identify, mainly due to their small size, but there is an up-to-date key. These insects are under recorded everywhere.

The order Dermaptera contains just 7 species in Britain. They are familiar to most people as earwigs. Forficula auricularia (left) [13mm] is the most commonly seen species. It occurs in most habitats and can even be found indoors. Despite having a bad reputation, this image shows an adult guarding eggs and recently hatched nymphs under the bark of a rotten tree trunk.

Parental care by the females is normal in the Dermaptera. The pincers are used in defence, to capture prey and courtship displays. This Labia minor (right) [6mm] was found in garden compost, a favoured habitat.

The order Odonata contains damselflies and dragonflies. They are the most recognisable order of insects around water. A number of species can be seen around garden ponds or the lakes and rivers in town parks. The Banded Demoiselle, Calopteryx splendens, [37mm] is a common species along urban rivers.

The Azure Damselfly, Coenagrion puella, [27mm] will visit garden ponds. There are a number of similar looking species in wet habitats. Some need a closer look to identify them correctly.

Some dragonflies, like this Southern Hawker, Aeshna cyanea, [56mm] can be found well away from water. They search far and wide for food which is caught on the wing. Some will eat their prey in the air, others can be spotted resting on the foliage of trees or shrubs.

There are around 49 species of Odonata in Britain. However, this number is increasing. Damselflies and dragonflies are benefitting from climate change. Many species new to Britain are appearing in counties along the south coast. Several species have established breeding populations in recent years. More are likely to follow. If you are interested in these insects, it is probably best to purchase a field guide that covers the European species as well as our own.

Moth Trapping

Most moth trapping is probably done in back gardens. Many moth recorders run their garden moth traps every night for most of the year. There are many different moth traps available commercially. You can buy mains operated versions for the garden or battery powered ones to take out to other habitats.

Several different types of lighting are used in moth traps. However, the type of light is less important than the type of trap. Also, high powered lights are not necessarily better than low powered ones. Only those species attracted to light will come to your trap no matter what type of light is being used. Many of these species will even be attracted to light from windows. Some years ago, I lived in an upstairs flat without access to a garden. I still managed to attract a good variety of insects simply by hanging a UV light in an open window. Insects can be found and recorded anywhere, anytime!

Some traps hold their catch better than others. This is the most important difference when choosing which type to use. The trap is a container over which the light is fixed. It will usually have something like egg cartons inside where specimens can hide. The standard method is to leave the trap running all night. Then, you look through the catch the next morning. Be aware that specimens can and do find their way out during the night and some will fly away quickly when the trap is opened. You could easily lose a prize specimen!

In pursuing your hobby, never think that you have to stick to traditional or standard methods. Do what best suits you, your intentions and your budget. I prefer to handle specimens as little as possible and only where necessary for identification. Moth wings are very easily damaged, other insects quickly lose legs or antennae.

I am not a regular moth trapper. When I do have a go, I prefer to set up the light without the trap. Moths and other insects will settle on a sheet hung behind the light. This way I can photograph specimens as they arrive and leave them be. Some moths will not readily settle, preferring to constantly flutter about. These can be netted and subdued in a killing jar, or the fridge if you prefer. Then, after taking photographs, they can be left to recover and fly off.

There are many species that are only weakly attracted to light and will not come directly to the trap. If you are asleep, you will not see these insects. If you stay up and watch the trap, look around the area with a torch. You will find many of these species sitting in the grass or on nearby foliage, or on fence posts etc.

If moths are your interest, it will be worth buying a few good books. There is not a single book that covers all our moths. All the macro-moths can be found in one book. It is possible to find the majority of the micro-moths spread across several books, but even then a good number will be missing. You will need to familiarise yourself with those species that can be identified from photographs.

Unfortunately, the rest can only be reliably identified by dissection. It is the standard method for identifying difficult moths. Records will not usually be accepted for these species without dissection having been carried out. I do not dissect and prefer to leave insects alive and free. Many enthusiasts these days do not want to molest the insects at all. That is perfectly understandable. Do not let anyone pressure you into going beyond what is comfortable for you. If all you wish to do is photograph without touching that is fine. There are many under-recorded species of insects that can be identified from good photographs if that is as far as you are willing to go. What is important is the accuracy of any records you submit. All good data is valuable.

Many of the moths I have seen and recorded have been at lights, usually a moth light in the garden. What follows is a selection of these moths. Hopefully, this selection will dispel the myth that moths are dull, drab insects.

Swift moths belong to the Hepialidae. This family is thought to have been around at the same time as the dinosaurs! This one is the Common Swift, Korscheltellus lupulina [17mm FWL].

Swift moths drop eggs into vegetation while flying, the larvae feed on plant roots. This is the Ghost Swift, Hepialus humuli [27mm FWL].

The December Moth, Poecilocampa populi, [18mm FWL] belongs to the Lasiocampidae. Males in this family have feather-like antennae. This species can be found in the autumn and winter months.

Hawkmoths belong to the Sphingidae. This Hummingbird Hawkmoth, Macroglossum stellatarum, [25mm FWL] was attracted to our kitchen light.

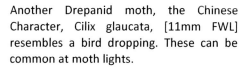

The Oak Hook-tip, Watsonella binaria, [16mm FWL] belongs to the Drepanidae family. The larvae feed mainly on oaks and the adults emerge twice each year.

Another Drepanid moth, the Chinese Character, Cilix glaucata, [11mm FWL] resembles a bird dropping. These can be common at moth lights.

The Peach Blossom, Thyatira batis, [18mm FWL] is easily identified. Its larvae feed on bramble in any habitat with trees and shrubs.

The Blood-vein, Timandra comae, [17mm FWL] belongs to the large Geometridae family. Many of them have a butterfly-like appearance when at rest.

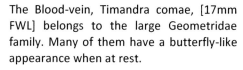

92

There are many carpet moths, so-called because of their patterns. The bright green colours of the Green Carpet, Colostygia pectinataria, [13mm FWL] very quickly fade to yellowish.

The pale-yellow Swallow-tailed Moth, Ourapteryx sambucaria, [28mm FWL] is one of our largest moth species.

The Dusky Thorn, Ennomos fuscantaria, [19mm FWL] is recognised by the darker edge to the forewings. There are several similar moths.

Waved Umber, Menophra abruptaria, [20mm FWL] larvae feed on Lilac and Garden Privet. Hence, they are commonly recorded in urban gardens.

The Light Emerald, Campaea margaritata, [20mm FWL] is one of a number of pale green Geometrid moths.

The larvae of the Clouded Silver, Lomographa temerata, [14mm FWL] can be found on garden fruit trees as well hedgerow shrubs.

The Lesser Swallow Prominent, Pheosia gnoma, [21mm FWL] belongs to the Notodontidae. The family name comes from the tooth-like projection seen sticking up from the edge of the wing.

The Sallow Kitten, Furcula furcula, [17mm FWL] is one of three similar species. This one is the commonest and a regular visitor to moth traps.

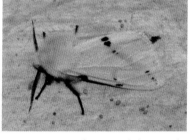

Over half our macro-moths belong to the Noctuidae family. Short-cloaked Moths, Nola cucullatella, [10mm FWL] are common garden insects with larvae feeding on hawthorns, Blackthorn and fruit trees.

The Buff Ermine, Spilosoma lutea, [19mm FWL] varies from yellowish to creamy-white. It is a common moth in most habitats.

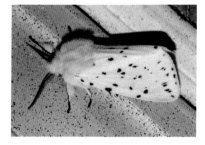

The White Ermine, Spilosoma lubricipeda, [20mm FWL] is also common. The larvae feed on a wide range of plants.

The Rosy Footman, Miltochrista miniata, [12mm FWL] is widespread but local. It can be found where there are mature hedgerows. This one came to a moth light in a friend's Sussex garden.

The Scarce Footman, Eilema complana, [16mm FWL] is one of several similar species. The larvae of footman moths mainly feed on lichens and are not easy to rear in captivity.

The Beautiful Hook-tip, Laspeyria flexula, [16mm FWL] can be found where there are mature trees. The larvae feed on lichens covering the branches.

The Burnished Brass, Diachrysia chrysitis, [19mm FWL] is the commonest of several similar species. This one came to floodlights on a road construction site.

The Marbled Beauty, Cryphia domestica, [12mm FWL] is a widespread species. It is commonly found in gardens and parks.

The Dusky Sallow, Eremobia ochroleuca, [16mm FWL] can be found in a variety of grassy habitats. The larvae feed on many grass species.

The larvae of Clouded-bordered Brindle, Apamea crenata, [20mm FWL] also feed on grasses. It particularly favours damper habitats but can be found in a variety of situations.

The Centre-barred Sallow, Atethemia centrago, [16mm FWL] can be found where there are ash trees growing. This one came to floodlights on a construction site.

The Barred Sallow, Tiliacea aurago, [17mm FWL] is found where there are Field Maple or Beech trees. This one was spotted in our lawn a few metres from the moth light.

Several of these Mervielle Du Jour, Griposia aprilina, [22mm FWL] were also spotted on the lawn. They did not come directly to the light.

The Varied Coronet, Hadena compta, [15mm FWL] was first known to breed in Britain in 1948. Its larvae will feed on Sweet-william, a common garden plant.

The Shuttle-shaped Dart, Agrotis puta, [15mm FWL] is common in a wide variety of habitats throughout Britain.

The Flame Shoulder, Ochropleura plecta, [15mm FWL] is also common and widespread. It can be quite numerous at moth lights.

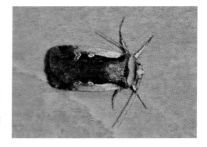

The Yponomeutidae includes a number of white moths with black spots. The Orchard Ermine, Yoponomeuta padella, [10mm FWL] is one of the commonest. The larvae can often be seen in large numbers in silk webs on hedgerows.

The Ypsolophidae has just 16 species. Ypsolopha dentella [10mm FWL] lays eggs on Honeysuckle in woods or gardens.

Ypsolopha sequella [9mm FWL] can be seen where there are Sycamores and Field Maples. It is common and widespread.

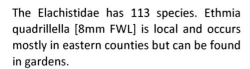

The Elachistidae has 113 species. Ethmia quadrillella [8mm FWL] is local and occurs mostly in eastern counties but can be found in gardens.

The Tortricidae has 399 species. The Large Fruit-tree Tortrix, Archips podana, [12mm FWL] is common in gardens. Its larvae can be found on many tree and shrub species.

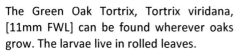

The Green Oak Tortrix, Tortrix viridana, [11mm FWL] can be found wherever oaks grow. The larvae live in rolled leaves.

The Garden Rose Tortrix, Acleris variegana, [8mm FWL] is also common in gardens. The larvae live in folded leaves, usually on roses, including garden varieties.

The Crambidae contains 145 species. The Garden Pebble, Evergestis forficalis, [14mm FWL] is a common garden visitor. The larvae feed on cabbages and related plants.

The Small Magpie, Anania hurtulata, [15mm FWL] is a common and distinctive moth. It can be found wherever Common Nettle grows.

Anania coronata [12mm FWL] is common in gardens south of Scotland. The larvae feed on garden shrubs such as Lilac and Garden Privet.

The Mother of Pearl, Pleuroptya ruralis, [16mm FWL] is another Common Nettle feeder found in urban habitats.

We have 44 species of Pterophoridae commonly known as plume moths. The White Plume Moth, Pterophorus pentadactyla, [14mm FWL] is one of the more common species.

Your light will attract much more than moths. There will be a range of species from a number of orders. Dung beetles, carrion beetles and some water bugs are regular visitors to light. Many of these unexpected visitors will not go into the trap and will be missed by the standard method. There are a number of large orange nocturnal parasitic wasps that will flutter about near the light then disappear into the darkness, only occasionally settling in the trap. Most of these wasp species are seriously under-recorded and will most likely be new to your area if you take the trouble to give them a go.

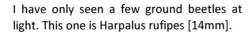

This Ilybius fuliginosus [11mm] is one of several water beetles that will come to light.

I have only seen a few ground beetles at light. This one is Harpalus rufipes [14mm].

This Hydrophilid beetle, Cercyon laminatus [3.5mm] was a nice surprise. It was the first seen in our county. It is covered with mites. Several species in the same genus are regular visitors to lights.

Dung beetles often come to light. Usually, they will be species from the Aphodiinae sub-family. This one, however, is Geotrupes spiniger [21mm] from the Geotrupidae.

The Cockchafer or Maybug, Melolontha melolontha [25mm] is a large beetle in the Melolonthinae sub-family. Their larvae feed on plant roots for three years. The adults will come to lights in buildings through open windows.

Nicrophorus humator [22mm] is a carrion beetle of the Silphidae family. It is commonly seen in moth traps. It is often covered with tiny mites.

Another nice surprise at my moth light was this Heterocerus fenestratus [4mm]. It belongs to the Heteroceridae, known as mud-loving beetles.

Lissonota biguttata [8mm] is a parasitic wasp in the Banchinae sub-family. What looks like a large sting is actually the egg laying tube or ovipositor.

Apechthis compunctor [10mm FWL] is in the Pimplinae sub-family. The short ovipositor with its down-curved tip is characteristic of the species.

Ophion slavecki [15mm FWL] is one of several orange-coloured nocturnal parasitic wasps. These impressive insects are common moth light intruders. The species need to be caught and examined for correct identification.

Netelia species can be mistaken for Ophions but they can be separated on wing vein structures. This one is Netelia testacea.

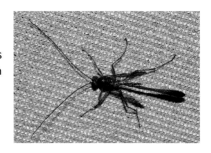

Mayflies belong to the Emphemeroptera order. They are usually associated with water. Some, like this Cloeon dipterum, [20mm WS] will come to lights.

Caddisflies belong to the Trichoptera order. They are also associated with water and most are nocturnal insects. This one is Holocentropus picicornis [7.5mm].

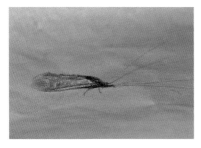

A number of species of caddisflies regularly turn up at moth lights. However, they are not always easy to identify. This one is Oecetis ochracea [11mm].

Farmland Safaris

Farmland comes in many different varieties. Most of the British landscape is farmed to greater or lesser degree. Even most of our woodlands are in fact trees being farmed! This section will focus on what most of us think of as farmland. That is, areas with well-defined field systems used for either crops or livestock. This is the most intensively farmed land and tends to have the poorest insect diversity.

Most of the crops grown in our countryside are varieties of grasses. These include staple foods such as wheat and barley. It also includes hay and silage for animal fodder. These fields are, in effect, larger versions of your garden lawn! Where they differ is in the management. These lawns are routinely sprayed with herbicides and pesticides that kill most of the wildflowers and their associated insects. This is not to say such fields hold no interest at all for the keen mini-beast hunter.

Most of the fields used for grazing livestock or growing hay and silage are planted with just one or two varieties of grass. All the wild grasses and any wildflowers are excluded. These fields are often sprayed with chemicals to make the grass grow quicker and to reduce pests. These 'improved' grasslands are heavily managed and are species poor. Even the dung produced by animals grazing these fields is of poor quality as far as the average dung beetle is concerned.

I live in dairy country and I am surrounded by silage fields. They are intensively managed to produce a number of silage crops each year. The herds are kept indoors and fed on the silage. This type of management leaves little room for any wildlife. If a field looks as green as the one shown here, then it probable has little wildlife value. The main interest for the bug hunter in these 'monoculture' fields is in the margins and hedgerows.

All is not lost though! There are still insects to be found even in these intensively managed fields. Try sweeping a net through a grass-based crop and it will catch a few insects. These might be bees, flies, beetles or the larvae of moths and sawflies. Try a suction sampler on the ground in a wheat field and you should still find a variety of ground beetles and bugs. The cowpats will still attract flies and a few beetle species. That is if you fancy a poke in the poo!

If you can find any older grazing meadows with a wider variety of grasses and other vegetation it will be home to a much greater diversity of insects. Neglected fields, paddocks and grassy corners can be particularly good. The field opposite has not been used for a couple of years and is now full of wildflowers.

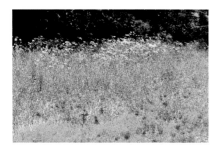

As your experience grows you will be able to spot a good habitat from a mile away. A neglected corner with tall white flowers should always be on the radar. These will be umbellifers such as Hogweed or Cow Parsley. They are always covered in a variety of insects, especially if they are in a sunny spot.

Where streams run or springs emerge, the ground is often too soft for modern heavy farm machinery. These areas can be neglected and full of life. Damp corners like these can be spotted by the change in vegetation. Instead of fodder grass or wheat there will be sedges, buttercups and Meadowsweet. Instead of hawthorn and oak there will be Alder and willows.

Despite decades of neglect and deliberate uprooting, we still have endless miles of hedgerows in our farmland. They are often comprised of a number of different tree and shrub species. This makes them more interesting than your average garden hedge. A good hedgerow will have hawthorn, Blackthorn, Elder, Holly and a scattering of mature trees such as oak and Ash. There will be other species dotted about too. Each tree and shrub species will be worth searching for its particular insect life. Try netting or beating the lower branches as far as you can reach. Check a local map to find footpaths and bridleways. These are often neglected and overgrown with the hedges cut less often. They can be real havens for wildlife.

Field margins are a type of edge habitat, similar to woodland edge but with mostly shrubs instead of trees. If a field has been ploughed right up to the base of the hedge, then this habitat has been lost. On the other hand, if a field has a margin of rough grass and other vegetation, then a variety of insects will be found. 'Set-aside' is the practice of deliberately leaving part of a field unploughed. This can be a strip down the middle or along the boundary. In set-aside areas wildflowers quickly take over. These will attract a lot of insects. They are particularly good places to find a range of bees and wasps. Your sweep net should be kept busy here.

The technique of 'tussocking' involves finding a tussock of grass and cutting it off at the base. The tussock is then broken up and sieved over a tray. Many insects will shelter in tussocks in poor weather or hibernate in them during the winter. Grasslands of different types and field margins are ideal places to try this method.

Farms where livestock are kept often have dung heaps. These can harbour a good selection of invertebrates. Bales of hay or straw that have been neglected for a while will also be good to search. These micro-habitats are particularly good when warm and full of fungi.

The best method is to sieve material into a tray. This will get rid of most of the larger debris leaving smaller debris and many insect specimens. You can either extract specimens straight into pots or take the mix home in a bag to search later.

Sadly, many farmland ponds were filled in decades ago to increase farm production. There are still some ponds around, but many are in poor condition. They will still be worth trying with a dipping net. Also, in livestock areas there will be water butts for the animals. These should not be overlooked, they too will be home to a few species of water bugs and beetles.

Farmyards and buildings can be home to a number of insect species. In particular, look out for a large variety of fly species. Many of these can be netted in flight around barns and stables without having to go inside. However, these are not really safe places to go mooching around in. If you want to take a look, ask the owner and take notice of what they tell you as regards the dangers and places to stay away from.

The verges along country lanes are not mown as often as they used to be. This has been a big boost to wildlife, especially insects. Overgrown verges with plants such as nettles, docks and umbellifers will always be worth sweeping. If the hedges are uncut then these too will be home to many species. Simply use a beating tray and stick. Be aware of passing traffic, even country lanes are busy these days.

Roadkill carrion is a really good micro-habitat. It is impossible to travel far along country lanes without finding a dead fox, badger or other animal. It may seem a bit gruesome, but there are a number of insects that are best found by looking at carcasses. If you are squeamish, just turn over a dead animal and see what is underneath. If you are not so easily shocked, you can take a piece of roadkill home. Put the carcass in container with holes that insects can get in. Check it each day to see what has turned up.

Entomologists have used many different methods for attracting insects to carcasses. I will not go into them here, they can be read about elsewhere. Most methods will produce results. I find that simply putting a piece of roadkill out of the road, say onto the verge, and checking each day works just fine. Why make life complicated? Any method will only attract species around the area at that time.

What follows is a selection of species I have recorded by searching in a variety of farmland habitats. As in all these sections, the selection is limited mainly by space.

The larvae of the White-letter Hairstreak, Satyrium w-album, live on the seeds and leaves of mature elms. These can be found in farmland hedgerows or woodlands.

The adults [13mm FWL] usually stay up in the trees, but they can sometimes be found on hedgerow brambles.

The Painted Lady, Vanessa cardui, [30mm FWL] lays eggs on thistles including those found along field margins. These migrants are more commonly seen in summer.

The Comma, Polygonia c-album, [26mm FWL] lays eggs on nettles or elms. The wing shape is unique in British butterflies. They can be common along field margins.

The larvae of the Comma writhe in a strange defensive display when disturbed.

The Gatekeeper, Pyronia tithonus, [20mm FWL] is a common hedgerow butterfly. This is a female. The male has a bar of brown scent scales across each forewing.

Hedgerows and field margins are good places to find moth larvae. This one is the Winter Moth, Operophtera brumata. This is one the most common larvae beaten from trees and shrubs in spring.

Elephant Hawkmoth larvae, Deilephila elpenor, are usually brown. Some, like this one, are green. They can be found on Rosebay Willowherb.

The White-spotted Pug larvae, Eupithecia tripunctaria, can be found in damper field margins on Elder in spring and umbellifers such as Wild Angelica in summer.

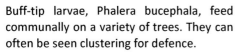

Buff-tip larvae, Phalera bucephala, feed communally on a variety of trees. They can often be seen clustering for defence.

Vapourer larvae, Orgyia antiqua, can be numerous on many tree and shrub species. This one has been infected by parasites.

Garden Tiger larvae, Arctia caja, have hairs that can cause rashes on human skin. They can be common, particularly on brambles and nettles.

Try setting up a moth light in a rough corner of a field and see what turns up. This is the Small Blood-vein moth, Scopula imitaria [12mm FWL]. It lives in small numbers in most habitats with bushes and trees.

The Peppered Moth, Biston betularia, [22mm FWL] lays eggs on many common plants. There is a black form called 'carbonaria' which is thought to be a reaction to pollution.

Buff-tip moths [22mm FWL] have a distinctive appearance. They will come to light or can be reared easily from larvae.

The Vapourer [12mm FWL] is more likely to be encountered by day but will come to light. The rarely seen females are flightless.

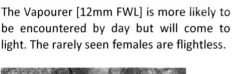

Winter Moth males [11mm FWL] are common at moth lights. The females, though, are wingless and rarely seen unless reared from larvae.

The Garden Tiger [25mm FWL] is more often seen in the larval stage. It can be reared easily from the older larvae found in the spring after hibernation.

Sweeping herbage along field edges will yield a number of micro-moth species. This one, Glyphipterix simpliciella, [4mm FWL] can be seen in numbers in buttercup flowers.

The Bird-cherry Ermine, Yponomeuta evonymella, [11mm FWL] comes to light and is common everywhere.

Esperia sulphurella [7mm FWL] flies by day and night. The larvae feed under the bark of decaying trees.

The larvae of Depressaria radiella can found in spinnings of silk in the flowers of umbellifers. They can be reared in captivity.

Agapeta hamana [10mm FWL] can be swept from herbage by day and will come to light. It is fairly common wherever there are thistles.

Many micro-moth larvae hide in leaves folded or spun with silk. It is worth checking a variety of foliage to see what you can find. This folded leaf on Dog Rose has been created by a larva of Notocelia cynosbatella.

Nephrotoma appendiculata [18mm FWL] is one of several black and yellow tiger craneflies. The larvae are pests feeding on the roots of grasses, including crops.

Nephrotoma flavescens is another tiger cranefly. The adults of these species are often seen at umbellifer flowers along field margins.

Tipula fascipennis is a distinctive cranefly species. It can be found along hedgerows and in rough grassland.

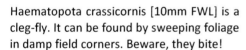

Haematopota crassicornis [10mm FWL] is a cleg-fly. It can be found by sweeping foliage in damp field corners. Beware, they bite!

Thereva nobilitata [14mm FWL] is a large fly that can also be swept from foliage around farmland habitats.

Leucozona leucorum [14mm FWL] is a striking hoverfly. It can be seen visiting flowers along hedgerows and is particularly common in May.

Myathropa florea [13mm FWL] larvae are aquatic. It is mainly a woodland species but will breed wherever there is water including cattle water butts.

Anomoia purmunda [4mm FWL] is a picture-winged fly. The females lay eggs on hawthorn berries in hedgerows.

The larvae of Hydromya dorsalis feed on aquatic snails. The adults can be swept from herbage in many habitats including hedgerows.

Scathophaga stercoraria [9mm FWL] is the common Yellow Dung Fly seen hovering around cowpats everywhere. The female is more green than yellow.

Mesembrina meridiana [12mm FWL] is commonly seen basking on foliage or fence posts in a range of habitats.

Stomoxys calcitrans [6mm FWL] is known as the Stablefly. The adults usually suck blood from farm animals but will also bite humans. The larvae live on decaying vegetation such as straw.

The Painted Mining Bee, Andrena fucata, [8mm FWL] prefers woodlands but can be found along hedgerows and in farmland copses. They nest in the ground singly or in groups.

This is Fabricius' Nomad Bee, Nomada fabriciana [7mm FWL]. It parasitises the nests of another bee, Andrena bicolor.

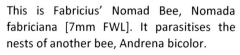

Oxybelus uniglumis [7mm] is a solitary wasp. The body pattern resembles that of numerous fly species. The wasp lays eggs on flies that are stung and buried in short burrows.

Earinus elator [7mm] is a parasitic wasp of the Braconidae. This one was swept from tree foliage on the edge of a copse.

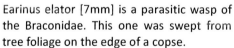

This cocoon was sifted from a grass tussock in a field margin during the winter. Finds like these are worth keeping until the adults emerge.

This Dusona recta emerged from the pupa above. Insects like this are often difficult to identify and are rarely recorded. This one was a new record for our county.

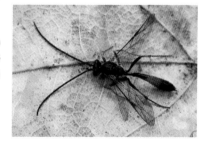

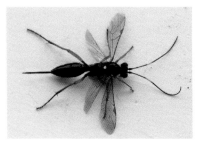

The Cryptinae is a sub-family of the Ichneumonidae. Species in this group can be difficult to identify due to the lack of resources. This Cryptus viduatorius [9mm] was swept from herbage along a field margin.

Ctenopelmatinae is another Ichneumonid sub-family. This species is Perilissus albitarsus. It was swept from a farmland hedgerow.

Many females in the Ichneumonidae hibernate over winter. Some, like this Ichneumon albiger, [9mm] can be found by tussocking.

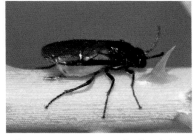

Some sawflies can be really common along hedgerows. This one is Arge pagana [9mm]. There are a number of very similar looking species.

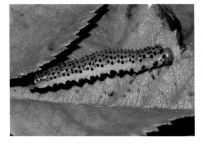

Many sawfly species use specific foodplants which can help to identify their larvae. Arge pagana uses Dog Rose.

Most sawfly larvae look like moth caterpillars. However, some look quite different. These slug-like larvae belong to Caliroa cerasi and were found on hawthorn.

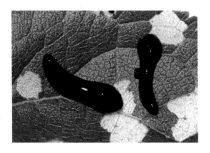

A number of water beetles can be found in farmland ponds. This Agabus sturmii [8mm] was found in pondweeds. Some species are more likely to be found in mud and debris on the pond bottom.

This Agabus bipustulatus [10.5mm] was found in a cattle water butt. There are 28 species in the Agabus and related Ilybius genres.

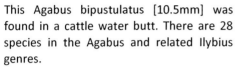

There are also 28 species in the Hydroporus genus. This Hydroporus palustris [3.7mm] was found by searching pond weeds.

Hydroporus beetles are small and can be hard to pick out. This Hydroporus planus [4.3mm] was found in a water butt full of algal mats.

Helophorus beetles are identified by the grooves on the pronotum. Helophorus grandis is the largest at about 7mm.

This weevil, Notaris scirpi, [6mm] was found in a Bulrush stem by a pond. A number of insect species can be found living or hibernating in such places.

114

Many ground beetles can be found in open farmland. Some, like this large Carabus nemoralis, [23mm] will hide under logs and bricks.

Others will be found in damp corners or next to streams. This Elaphrus riparius [6mm] was found on the mud of a flood pond.

Some ground beetles have more unusual habitats. Clivina fossor [6.4mm] lives like a mole tunnelling under the ground. This one was found when I was digging holes to plant trees.

Quite a few species in the Bembidion genus can be found around wet areas. This Bembidion varium [4.6mm] was found on mud.

Leistus ferrugineus [7mm] is a wingless species. This one was found under a brick in a wet copse.

As well as being found on the ground, adults of the Ophonus genus will climb vegetation to eat seeds. This one is Ophonus rufibarbis [8mm].

Sifting grass tussocks in field margins is a good way to find many species, especially rove beetles. The tiny Metopsia clypeata [2.8mm] is easily overlooked in a tray full of grass sievings.

Tachyporus hypnorum [3.5mm] is one of a number of teardrop-shaped rove beetles. Many are difficult to identify.

Deleaster dichrous [6.8mm] is distinctive and unmistakeable. It is usually associated with streams. I have found it in tussocks and under logs by running water.

Anotylus rugosus [4.8mm] can be found in many habitats especially where it is damp. There are a few similar species, but they can be identified with a hand lens.

Paederus riparius [8mm] can be found in wet neglected field corners. This species has yellow jaws. There is a similar species with black jaws.

Ocypus olens, [28mm] often known as the Devil's Coach-horse, is a large rove beetle. It preys on other invertebrates, including some of our largest ground beetles.

Beetles can be found in all macro and micro habitats in farmland. This Trox scaber [7mm] was found in an old jackdaw's nest in a fallen Beech tree.

This colourful rove beetle, Platydracus stercorarius, [14mm] was found running across a country lane.

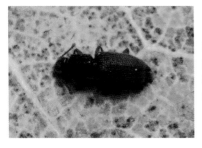

Decaying hay bales will yield many small species like this Monotoma bicolor [2.2mm]. Simply sift handfuls of hay into a tray. Look out for pseudoscorpions too!

Endomychus coccineus [5mm] looks like a ladybird but is unrelated. A cluster of these was found under the bark of a dead hedgerow Beech.

This Mycetophagus quadripustulatus [5.5mm] was found in a Polyporus squamosus fungi on a fallen Beech trunk.

Lots of species can be found by simply sweeping the vegetation along the hedgerows. This Cassida rubiginosa [7mm] was netted from thistles on a strip of set-aside.

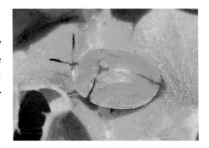

If you have the stomach for it, a number of beetles can be found on dead animals. Margarinotus brunneus [7.5mm] is one of several species of the Histeridae associated with carrion.

Beetles of the Silphidae are the real carrion specialists. This one is the unmistakable Oiceoptoma thoracicum [14mm].

Species in the genus Nicrophorus are known as burying or sexton beetles. Nicrophorus vespilloides [15mm] is one of several large black and orange species.

Rove beetles are common in carrion. Many will be eating things such as fly larvae rather than the carrion itself. This one is Phloeonomus punctipennis [1.8mm].

Necrobia violacea [4.5mm] is in the Cleridae family, known as chequered beetles. This species tends to be found on carcasses in a late stage of decay or even on dry bones.

Omosita discoidea [2.9mm] in the Nitidulidae, also comes to older carcasses. It can also be found in haystack litter. Species of the Nitidulidae are known as sap beetles.

118

Aradus depressus [5.5mm] is in the Aradidae family of flatbugs. They can be seen under the bark of trees, including hedgerow oaks where this one was found.

The Pied Shield Bug, Tritomegas bicolor, [6.5mm] is a distinctive species. They can be found in numbers in field margins where deadnettles grow in profusion.

The Bishop's Mitre, Aelia acuminata, [8.5mm] can be found by sweeping rough grassy patches including those found along field margins.

Grypocoris stysi [7mm] is usually found on nettles in wooded areas. This one was found in a farmland copse.

Gerris odontogaster [8mm] is one of a number of pond skater species. This one was dipped from a water butt.

Notonecta maculata [18mm] is one of our four backswimmers. This one was dipped from a farmland pond.

Macustus grisescens [5.5mm] is a common species in the Cicadellidae. It can be found in large numbers by sweeping most grassy areas. They will also turn up in suction samples.

The aphid Ceruraphis eriophori [2.4mm] can be found on viburnum species in most habitats. These were in a damp field corner.

The springtail, Dicyrtomina saundersi, [3mm] is a common species found under stones and logs everywhere.

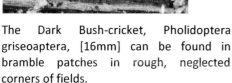

The Dark Bush-cricket, Pholidoptera griseoaptera, [16mm] can be found in bramble patches in rough, neglected corners of fields.

The scorpion-fly, Panorpa germanica, [13mm FWL] is a voracious predator of other insects. It can be swept from vegetation along hedgerows.

The strange looking Dilta hibernica belongs to the order Archaeognatha. They are primitive insects and not often recorded. They can be found, as this one was, by sieving leaf litter from beneath hedgerows.

Open Land Safaris

Open land is land with only small numbers of trees and bushes. This is as opposed to woodland or scrub where the main vegetation is trees and shrubs. Most farmland is 'open'. Our other main types of open land are usually more diverse than the open farmland discussed in the previous section. The focus here will mainly be on grasslands, heathlands and moorlands.

What is the difference between grassland, heathland and moorland? The obvious answer might be that the vegetation is different. This is partly true but there are underlying reasons for this difference in vegetation. The best grasslands tend be found in areas where the underlying rocks are chalks or limestones. There are small wildflower meadows dotted about elsewhere, but they are not quite the same. Heathlands tend to develop on low lying sandstones and are often quite dry. Moorlands tend to develop at higher altitudes on granites or gritstones and are often damp or wet.

Grasslands

Grasslands on chalk or limestone are known as 'calcareous'. The most diverse grasslands have never been ploughed or sprayed and are not over-grazed by sheep. Such grasslands are known as 'unimproved'. Some of the best examples are in places such as the Cotswolds, South Downs, Chilterns and the dales of Derbyshire and Yorkshire. Calcareous grasslands are probably the only land-based habitat we have with a diversity of species close to that of ancient oak woodland.

Aston Rowant is a fine example of chalk grassland. It is in the Chilterns, East of Oxford and is managed by Natural England as a National Nature Reserve. The grassland is grazed by sheep, but careful management ensures that a wide variety of wildflowers grows there.

Lathkill Dale is a limestone valley in the Derbyshire Dales, again managed by Natural England. The upper end of the valley is mostly grassland. Here, good management and the rocky terrain ensure a diversity of plants and associated insects.

Chalk and limestone areas in Britain are often quarried for stone, some emerge as sea cliffs. These areas can be even more diverse than the grasslands due to the lack of grazing. The cliffs shown here are at the back of Tout Quarry nature reserve on the Isle of Portland.

Please note that chalk and limestone grasslands are home to many rare and delicate plants, including many of our orchids. Do not just go trampling all over the area you are visiting. Stick to paths or sheep trails where possible and watch what is under your feet! Be cautious around unfenced cliffs.

Sand dunes are a particular type of grassland dominated by marram grasses. Most of our dune systems have been spoiled by tourism developments and encroachment of scrub. A few of the larger areas are now nature reserves with a fantastic diversity of sand dune insects.

Heathlands

Whereas grasslands have a high plant diversity, heathlands can seem quite poor. Some heathlands are dominated by Heather and Bilberry, while grasses can be more dominant on other heaths. Most heathlands will also have a scattering of trees, especially Silver Birch and Scots Pine or Silver Fir. Gorse and Broom are present on some heathlands and these have their own associated insects.

Prees Heath and Prees Heath Common managed by Shropshire Wildlife Trust and Butterfly Conservation is a heathland in the making. Part of it is dominated by Heather. Though it is ecologically a heathland, it can also be classed as brownfield. It was used as an airfield during World War II. Many heathlands have been used by man in the past.

122

Highgate Common, managed by Staffordshire Wildlife Trust, is a lowland heath with as much grass as Heather. There is also some gorse and Broom along with hawthorn, Rowan, oaks and other trees scattered about the open areas. It is one of the best heathlands in the Midlands.

The most diverse lowland heaths are in Dorset and Sussex. Most are now nature reserves, but the trusts usually welcome amateur entomologists. In return for a report of your findings they will provide permissions. The heath shown here is Iping Common in West Sussex.

Many of our lowland conifer plantations are on former heathlands. When blocks of trees are clear felled the land temporarily returns to heath. These transitional habitats can be quite diverse with the range of species changing over a few years as the new trees grow. This image is part of Cannock Chase in Staffordshire.

Moorlands

If you visit upland parts of the west or north of Britain you will find habitats that resemble heathlands. These are moorlands. They are distinctly different to heathlands. The uplands are wetter and colder, and the underlying rocks acidify the soils. The conditions are harsh with plants and insects adapted to survive where many lowland species could not.

On some moorlands heathers are dominant. This is what gives them the appearance of heathland. The grasses will be different from those on heathland and gorse and Broom are not usually present. There will be more sedges and rushes and trees are more likely to be Rowan. This different range of plant life will give rise to a different range of insects.

The moorland in the previous two images is Knotbury Common in Staffordshire. This is a relatively small with roads nearby. However, in Wales, the north of England and Scotland, there are vast areas of moorland without roads or settlements. These places can be rather dangerous. The weather can turn nasty very quickly, it is then easy to get lost. There are peat bogs and rocky outcrops that disappear in sudden mists making them impossible to see. These moorlands are fascinating places to visit, but always do so safely. Make sure you have local maps and wear suitable clothing.

Searching in open habitats

Most of the vegetation in open habitats is low growing and should be swept with a suitable net. Tougher plants can be tapped into a tray. Remember to sample all species of plants and different plant assemblages. Many of the wildflowers will have their own insect species. There are likely to be many types of flying insects such as various Diptera and Hymenoptera. If you are

interested in any of these, they will need to be potted from a net, quickly. Everything else, including many species of Coleoptera and Hemiptera, can be tipped into a tray to select out any interesting specimens.

Heathers and Bilberry are home to many species of moths, especially micro-moths. If you are able to provide fresh food on a daily basis, it is worth trying to rear some of their larvae. Do not take too many of any one species though.

The ground itself will be home to many species across many insect families. These are mostly insects that either run on the ground or live among the bases and roots of the plants. Most of them rarely climb the vegetation and will not be caught in a sweep net. These species can be found by hand-eye searching. This method will turn up a few specimens, but it is not the most productive way to find insects. You can try pulling up dead plant litter from around the plant bases and putting it in tray. Try not to damage living plants, though. If you are able to re-visit the site, you could set pitfall traps. These can be more effective but require a bit more planning and time for re-visits to collect the catch. The best method, though, is to use your suction sampler and a tray.

Do not forget to check any trees or shrubs in the area. There will be many resident species that can be beaten from the foliage. They may also provide refuges for species just passing through the open areas.

Most of the vegetation in sand dunes is quite tough. Marram grasses, in particular, will cut human skin with ease. Shorts are not a good option, even if the sun is shining. Sweep net and suction sampler are very useful here. However, micro-habitats include the marram roots below the sand and the underside of driftwood and piles of rotting seaweed. Remember to respect

the habitat, sand dunes are very delicate and easily damaged. Also, watch for rare plants, such as orchids, under your feet.

One of the best micro-habitats in open areas is dung. Heathlands are often grazed by cattle or ponies. The cattle dung is usually a better quality than that found on farmland grazing. It tends to be drier and looks more like horse dung. Grasslands can be grazed by cattle or sheep. Moorlands are more likely to be grazed by sheep alone. Lowland heaths are often used by dog walkers where dog poo will be used by a few species. The best way to search dung is to use a stick or other implement to break up the dung and use tweezers to extract specimens. Beetles can also be washed out of dung in a bucket of water.

What follows is a selection of species I have found and recorded in a variety of open habitats. This selection represents a fraction of the species I have found in these species rich ecosystems.

Skipper butterflies are most usually found in open places. The Essex Skipper, Thymelicus lineola, [12mm FWL] is one several orange species found in flower rich grasslands.

The Green Hairstreak, Callophrys rubi, [13mm FWL] prefers heathland where heathers and gorse are used by their larvae.

Most of our blue butterflies also prefer flower rich grasslands. The larvae of some species, like this Chalkhill Blue, Polyommatus coridon, [17mm FWL] are associated with ants.

Many of our fritillary butterflies lay eggs on violets. The large Dark Green Fritillary, Speyeria aglaja, [29mm FWL] can be seen on grasslands and heathlands.

Despite its name, the Marbled White, Melanargia galathea, [25mm FWL] is in the brown butterfly family. The female fires eggs into deep grass while flying.

The Grayling, Hipparchia semele, [26mm FWL] is also a brown butterfly. It is most commonly found on heaths in the south or in sand dunes around the coast.

126

Some of our day-flying moths have colours that warn that they are poisonous. This one is the Five-spot Burnet, Zygaena trifolii [12mm FWL]. It can be found on southern grasslands where it feeds on trefoils.

The Emperor Moth, Saturnia pavonia, [22mm FWL] is commonly found on heathlands. The larvae mainly feed on heathers and are easy to rear in captivity.

The Small Elephant Hawkmoth, Deilephila porcellus, [20mm FWL] is most common on calcareous grasslands. The larvae feed mainly on bedstraws.

The Purple Bar, Cosmorhoe ocellata, [10mm FWL] also lays eggs on bedstraws. It can be found in a variety of open habitats.

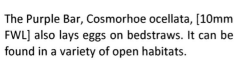

The Chalk Carpet, Scotopteryx bipunctaria, [15mm FWL] has a restricted distribution. It can be disturbed by day in rough chalky places and old quarries by the coast.

The Common Heath, Ematurga atomaria, [11mm FWL] can be seen on heaths and other open areas. They fly by day. The males have feather-like antennae.

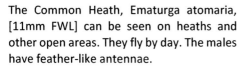

The Clouded Buff, Diacrisia sannio, [19mm FWL] can be found in most open habitats. The male can be disturbed by day and is mainly yellow. The rarely seen female is more orange.

The Scarlet Tiger, Callimorpha dominula, [22mm FWL] flies by day in the south of Britain. It can be found in most open habitats with a preference for damp grasslands and coastal cliffs.

The Cinnabar Moth, Tyria jacobaeae, [16mm FWL] is also a day-flying species. The brown and yellow larvae feeding on Ragwort are probably more familiar than the adults.

The Burnet Companion, Euclidia glyphica, [12mm FWL] can be seen during the day in rough grassy places.

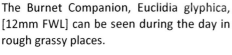

Mother Shipton, Euclidia mi, [12mm FWL] is often seen with the previous species. They fly in the same habitats from May to July.

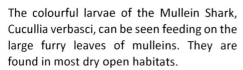

The colourful larvae of the Mullein Shark, Cucullia verbasci, can be seen feeding on the large furry leaves of mulleins. They are found in most dry open habitats.

The Momphidae contains 15 species, most of them are found in open habitats. Mompha locupletella [5mm FWL] prefers damper areas with willowherbs.

Aethes beatricella [8mm FWL] is a tortrix species. It lays eggs on Hemlock and Alexanders in rough open places.

Philedonides lunana [6mm FWL] lives on heathlands and moorlands. Males can be seen around heather during the day.

Dichrorampha alpinana [7mm FWL] is a common species, especially on calcareous grasslands. The adults are seen visiting flowers during the day.

The Crescent Plume, Marasmarcha lunaedactyla, [10mm FWL] can be found on downland, sand dunes, chalk quarries and sea-cliffs in the south of England.

Pempelia palumbella [12mm FWL] is a local species found on heathlands and cliffs with Heather. The larvae feed on heathers.

Bibio pomonae, sometimes known as the Red-thighed St Mark's fly or Heather Fly, is a distinctive member of its genus. This one was found on moorland in Wales.

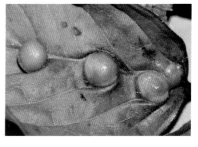

Remember to look for galls. These galls are caused by the fly Craneiobia corni on Dogwood. These were found at Cissbury Ring in Sussex.

Stratiomys potamida [10mm FWL] is one of several similar soldier-flies. The larvae live in water, but the adults can be seen on umbellifers. Look for them around wet areas of heaths.

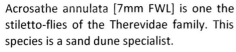

Acrosathe annulata [7mm FWL] is one the stiletto-flies of the Therevidae family. This species is a sand dune specialist.

Dysmachus trigonus [10mm FWL] is a robber-fly of the Asilidae family. It is associated with sandy heaths and coasts.

Leptogaster cylindrica [6mm FWL] is another robber-fly. This species is associated with rough grassy habitats such as Aston Rowant where this specimen was found.

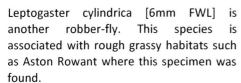

130

Gymnosoma rotundatum [6mm FWL] is in the Tachindae family. It is restricted to the southeast and can be found on dry heaths and downs. The larvae are parasites of shieldbugs.

Hoverflies are well represented in open habitats. Chrysotoxum bicinctum [12mm FWL] is a widespread species on grasslands.

Chrysotoxum elegans [11mm FWL] is one several similar species. This one is scarce and only found on chalklands and coasts in the south.

Platycheirus granditarsus [7mm FWL] is from a large genus. This is one of the easier members to identify. It is found near water in open habitats.

Picture-winged flies of the Tephritidae are common in open habitats. Urophora jaceana [7mm FWL] causes galls on Common Knapweed in grasslands.

Merzomyia westermannia is another picture-winged fly. This one was found on chalk downland at Cissbury Ring.

Damselflies are associated with water. The Small Red Damselfly, Ceriagrion tenellum, [25mm] prefers acidic bog pools on heathlands and moors. This one was seen on a Dorset heath.

The Golden-ringed Dragonfly, Cordulegaster boltonii, [59mm] prefers streams on heathlands and moors. This specimen is eating a bee.

Many dragonflies are sexually dimorphic. The female Keeled Skimmer, Orthetrum coerulescens, [28mm] is a golden yellow insect.

Fresh male Keeled Skimmers are yellow and black. As they mature they turn blue. This species can be seen flying over the heathers on southern heaths.

Grasshoppers are common in most open habitats. The Stripe-winged Grasshopper, Stenobothrus lineatus, [18mm] is usually found in the south of England.

Long-winged Coneheads, Conocephalus discolor, [19mm] appeared in Britain in the 1930s. Since then, they have colonised rank grasslands across much of England.

Beetles are very well represented in open habitats. The Green Tiger Beetle, Cicindela campestris, [15mm] can be seen running on the bare sandy ground of heathlands. The larvae are ambush predators living in burrows.

Dune Tiger Beetles, Cicindela maritima, [13mm] can be seen running in sand dunes. Like all tiger beetles, they fly off quickly when disturbed.

Brachinus crepitans [8mm] is a scarce ground beetle. It is found on calcareous grasslands, usually near the south coast. These were found in Tout Quarry on Portland.

Broscus cephalotes [20mm] is a large ground beetle. It is usually found at the coast, often hiding under driftwood on sandy beaches.

Bembidion iricolor [5mm] is also a coastal species. It is often found under rotting seaweed on bare sand.

Pogonus chalceus [7mm] is one of three species in a genus associated with open salt marshes. This one, however, was found in a damp area in sand dunes.

Dicheirotrichus obsoletus [7mm] is also found on salt marshes and in damp dunes. It occurs mainly along the south coast but can also be found at Morfa Dyffryn.

Calathus cinctus [7.3mm] can be found on dry sandy soils at the coast or on heathlands. They like to hide under stones and logs.

The rare Cymindis axillaris [9.5mm] can be found under stones and at plant roots on dry heaths and grasslands in the south and east.

Harpalus rubripes [10.5mm] is one of many species in the same genus that inhabit open habitats. This species prefers sandy heaths and gravelly soils.

Silpha laevigata [15mm] is a scarce beetle of dry stony places near the coast. It is a predator of snails.

Drusilla caniliculata [5mm] is a rove beetle that can be found on heathland. This specimen was found by sieving litter from under Heather.

134

Cafius xantholoma [8mm] is a rove beetle associated with rotting seaweed on sandy beaches. This specimen was found in seaweed under driftwood.

Ocypus aeneocephalus [13mm] is found in most damp open habitats. This one was found in wet moss on moorland by suction sampling.

Aegialia arenaria [6mm] is a small relative of the dung beetles. This species, though, can be found running on bare sand or at plant roots in dunes.

Anomalia dubia [13mm] is a large chafer beetle, also related to dung beetles and is found in sand dunes. On hot days, many specimens can be found dead on the sand.

Cetonia aurata [18mm] is another large chafer beetle. They can be seen on flowers in grassy places in southern counties.

Dascillus cervinus, [10mm] sometimes known as the Orchid Beetle, can be found in the north and west of Britain. It prefers calcareous soils and is often seen resting on foliage or sometimes visiting flowers.

Byrrhus pilula [8mm] is one of several pill beetles. This species can be found on sandy or stony soils such as heaths. They are often found by sieving damp moss or litter.

Agrypnus murinus [15mm] is a distinctive click beetle. It can be swept from vegetation in grasslands.

Selatosomus aeneus [14mm] is a scarce click beetle. It is found under stones on heaths and rough grasslands. This one was found in the entrance to a rabbit burrow by suction sampling in the Malvern Hills.

This is a larva of the Glow-worm, Lampyris noctiluca [11mm]. Adult males have luminescent patches that glow in the dark. This species is found on calcareous grasslands and dunes.

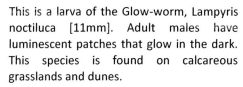

Cantharis nigricans [10mm] can be swept from vegetation in many open habitats including rough grasslands.

Psilothrix viridicoerulea [6mm] is in the Melyridae family. They can be found at flowers in grassy places, often at the coast.

The Heather Ladybird, Chilocorus bipustulatus, [3.5mm] can be found on heaths with abundant Heather. They can be found by sweeping, but it is better to tap clumps of Heather into a tray.

The Hieroglyph Ladybird, Coccinella hieroglyphica, [4.5mm] is another scarce species found on heaths and moors with Heather.

Lagria hirta [9mm] is a common Tenebrid beetle. It is associated with flowers and can be found on heathlands and grasslands with scattered trees and shrubs.

Phylan gibbus [7.5mm] is a Tenebrid beetle found running on bare sand. It is a scarce species but can be found in most of our large dune systems.

Cteniopus sulphureus [6.5mm] is a local species. It can be swept from flowers on sandy soils, especially at the coast.

Anthicus bimaculatus [3.5mm] is one of the ant-like flower beetles. It can be found on sandy soils at the coast, but it is well camouflaged and hard to spot.

Notoxus monoceros [4.6mm] has a distinctively shaped pronotum. It can be found in litter or at flowers on dry sandy soils.

Cryptocephalus aureolus [6mm] is one of 20 pot beetle species. This one can be swept from yellow flowers such as buttercups.

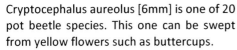

Timarcha tenebricosa, [15mm] also known as the Bloody-nosed Beetle, is a common species feeding on bedstraws in grasslands.

Calomicrus circumfusus [3.5mm] is a scarce leaf beetle species. It is associated with gorse on heathlands. This one was seen at Arne in Dorset.

Sermylassa halensis [5.8mm] feeds on bedstraws. It is found on open grasslands, particularly on calcareous soils. These were spotted in Lathkill Dale.

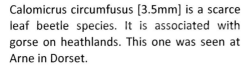

Neocrepidodera transversa [4.5mm] is one of many flea beetles. This species can be swept from vegetation in open habitats across most of Britain.

Cassida flaveola [5mm] is a tortoise beetle found in grasslands. It can be swept from vegetation during the summer or sieved from grass litter in the winter months.

Exapion ulicis [2.3mm] is one of several similar weevil species. This one can be found on gorse, especially on heathlands.

Many weevils feed on specific plants. Malvapion malvae [2.1mm] lives only on Common Mallow, often in grasslands.

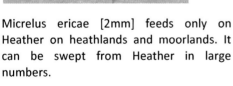

Micrelus ericae [2mm] feeds only on Heather on heathlands and moorlands. It can be swept from Heather in large numbers.

Hypera nigrirostris [3.8mm] feeds on Red Clover in grasslands. This one was found running on bare sand in dunes.

The larvae of Pissodes castaneus [6.3mm] live in the wood of dead and dying pine trees. This one was beaten from a pine tree on heathland.

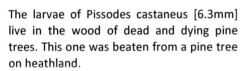

Beetles from a number of different families are commonly found in dung. Sphaeridium scarabaeoides [6mm] is one of several similar species in the same genus. The larvae eat fly grubs in dung.

A number of hister beetles are found in dung. Hypocaccus dimidiatus [4.3mm] occurs in dung on sandy coasts and dunes.

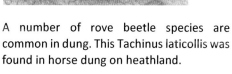

Another hister beetle, Margarinotus purpurascens, [4mm] is found in dung at inland sites. It is a scarce species.

A number of rove beetle species are common in dung. This Tachinus laticollis was found in horse dung on heathland.

Philonthus marginatus [8mm] is one the more distinctive species of rove beetle in dung. This one was found in a badger latrine.

Ontholestes murinus [12mm] is another distinctive species. This one was found in a dry-ish cow dung on a heathland.

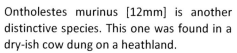

Dor beetles belong to the Geotrupidae family. They are all large dung beetles. Perhaps the most spectacular is the male Typhaeus typhoeus [18mm] with three horns on its pronotum. They prefer sand or chalk soils because they dig deep burrows.

Most true dung beetles belong to the Aphodiini tribe. Acrossus luridus [7.5mm] prefers sheep or cow dung.

Agroliinus lapponum [6mm] prefers sheep dung. It is restricted to the north and west of Britain.

Aphodius foetidus [7mm] prefers sandy soils. It can be found in decaying vegetation as well as dung.

Rhodaphodius foetens [8mm] prefers drying cattle dung. It is more common in the south of Britain. It can be separated from similar red species by its orange underside.

Onthophagus coenobita [8mm] is one of several related species that can be found in dog poo. They prefer dry heaths and grasslands.

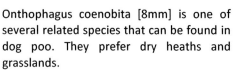

Bees and wasps like sunshine so it is no surprise to find many species in open habitats. Colletes cunicularius [10mm FWL] is a rare bee found mainly in dunes at the coast. It can be seen in large numbers where it does occur.

Gorytes quadrifasciatus [10mm] is one of many black and yellow solitary wasps found on heaths and other sandy places. They dig burrows to stock with prey for their larvae.

Ants are familiar insects in open habitats. Lasius flavus [4mm] is particularly common in grasslands where it creates nest mounds.

Spider-hunting wasps dig burrows in sand and stock them with spiders. They can be seen on sandy heaths and dunes. This one is Pompilius cinereus [6mm FWL].

Cuckoo wasps of the Chrysididae family lay eggs in the nests of other insects. There are a lot of species, all are difficult to identify. This Elampus panzer [6mm] was swept from umbellifers on a Midlands heathland.

Macrocentrus thoracicus is a parasitic Braconid wasp. This one was swept from herbage on a heathland. There are many related species, all are under-recorded.

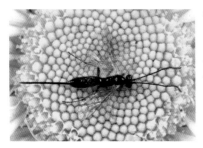

Glypta trochanterata is parasitic wasp in the Banchinae sub-family. There are many related species, but they can be identified with a key. Many, like this one, can be swept from vegetation in open areas.

Amblyteles armatorius [14mm] is one of the more colourful Ichneumonid wasps. They are seen on umbellifers in open areas such as grasslands.

Ichneumonid species from many genres can be found on umbellifers. This Vulgichneumon maculicauda [12mm] was found on heathland.

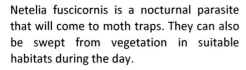

Netelia fuscicornis is a nocturnal parasite that will come to moth traps. They can also be swept from vegetation in suitable habitats during the day.

Sawflies are also common in open habitats. This Tenthredopsis ornata [9mm] was swept from herbage on a moorland.

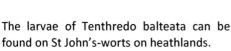

The larvae of Tenthredo balteata can be found on St John's-worts on heathlands.

Bugs from most families are common in open habitats, especially those associated with flowers or the ground. This Neottiglossa pusilla [4.3mm] was found in the grasslands of the Malvern Hills.

The Gorse Shieldbug, Piezodorus lituratus, [12mm] lives on gorse. It is a common bug found on heathlands.

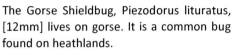

The Turtle Bug, Podops inuncta, [5.5mm] lives on grasses. This one was found under a stone in an overgrown limestone quarry.

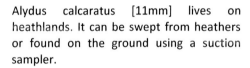

Alydus calcaratus [11mm] lives on heathlands. It can be swept from heathers or found on the ground using a suction sampler.

Megalonotus chiragra [5mm] lives on the ground. It can be found by suction sampling or pitfall trapping on grasslands and chalk downlands.

Peritrechus lundii [4.5mm] also lives on the ground on grasslands, heaths and dunes. There are many similar looking species in the same habitats.

Berytinus minor [6mm] is a stiltbug in the Berytidae family. It prefers grassy habitats, including the grassier parts of heaths where this specimen was found.

Another Berytid, Neides tipularius [11mm] is found in dry habitats. This specimen was spotted on the ground in sand dunes.

Pithanus maerkelii [4.5mm] is a common mirid bug. It prefers damp grassy habitats. This specimen was swept from moorland grasses.

Neophilaenus campestris [5.5mm] belongs to the Aphrophoridae family. It can be found by sweeping in grassy places as far north as Yorkshire.

Ulopa reticulata [3mm] is the commoner of two related species. This one lives only on heathers. It is usually to be found at the plant bases.

Aphids can be numerous in open habitats. This one is Cinara pinea [4mm]. It can be found by beating pines including those found scattered around heathlands.

Woodland Safaris

A woodland is just a block of trees, right? On the surface, yes, this is true. However, take a deeper look and you will find one of our most complex and diverse ecosystems. Examples of most of our insect families can be found in woodlands. This should not be a surprise, woodland is the natural habitat of our islands. It is the habitat most of our insects have evolved to live in.

Trees are the most obvious organisms in a woodland. The types, ages and number of trees in a woodland will shape the rest of the ecosystem and determine the extent of its insect diversity. Possibly the most important organisms in a woodland, though, are fungi. Most fungi are hidden from view most of the time. Yet, without them, the woodland ecosystem would not survive. Fungi are as interesting to the mini-beast hunter as the trees they live amongst as we will see later.

It is useful to get to know the commoner trees by sight. Most of the tree species you will see are not actually native to Britain. However, most of the broadleaved trees have been here a long time and many of our insects have adapted to make use of them. Most of the conifers, on the other hand, are more recent introductions and very few of our insects make use of them.

The most important trees to look for, if you want to find a good range of insects, are oaks, elms and birches. These trees provide food and homes for large numbers of our insects. Other trees will have fewer associated species. Young block plantations, even of broadleaved trees, will usually have only a small range of insect species. This is because the ecosystem has had little time to develop. The range is also reduced in dense blocks of older trees. This is because dense stands of trees, whatever their ages, have a poorer ground flora and fewer micro-habitats.

The greatest diversity is to be found in ancient woodlands with a range of tree species of differing ages. There should be saplings, old trees full of rot holes and all ages in between. There should be gaps where trees have fallen, allowing light to penetrate to the woodland floor, and plenty of dead wood lying around.

Ebernoe Common in Sussex, shown here, is a good example of a diverse woodland.

An ancient woodland, such as Brocton Coppice shown here, has distinct layers, each layer is a macro-habitat in its own right. Firstly, the 'ground layer' will usually have a range of vegetation. This can be carpets of woodland flowers such as Bluebells, Primroses and Lesser Celandines. In more shaded areas it might be carpets of mosses and ferns. The ground flora will largely be determined by soil type and shade. Whatever the case may be, the ground flora will attract a variety of insects. Even dense carpets of Bracken have their own range of associated species.

The ground itself should be alive with insects. They are not always easily seen though. Look for areas with dense leaf litter. Leaf litter that is old and affected by fungi is particularly productive. Use a suction sampler or sieve handfuls into a tray and wait a minute for things to stir. There are insects that live on the rotting leaves, insects that feed on the fungi and, of course, insects that feed on insects. Leaf litter is like a whole undiscovered world. There will be ground beetles and bugs under logs, along with a range of other invertebrates such as woodlice and spiders. Turn the logs back over when you have finished looking to preserve the habitat and its inhabitants.

Dead wood has its own set of associated insects, many of which require there to be fungi present. The fungi in this 'fungoid wood' are not always obvious, they may not be in the form of visible toadstools. Tree stumps and fallen trees rotted by fungi can be searched for a range of species. Look under loose bark or dig a little into the rotted wood. As well as adults there will be many

beetle larvae. It is preferable to leave these covered up when you have done. Larvae will burrow back into the wood or bark and continue their development.

Old oak trees go through a rot process that can take hundreds of years. The heartwood often turns red, as shown here. When a tree falls this red-rot wood is exposed and accessible. It can be home to many rare and interesting species.

Woodpeckers will often reveal the presence of wood boring species as they look for grubs and larvae to eat. Sometimes, exposed larvae can be reared to obtain adult beetle specimens.

A number of fungi will attract insects. The two most productive are Birch Polypore (Piptoporus betulinus), shown left, and Chicken-of-the-Woods (Laetiporus sulphureus), shown right. Both fungi will attract different species as they mature. They are both fairly common, but do not destroy every fungus looking for specimens. It is important to leave a good supply for the insects.

The 'understorey' layer is usually composed of smaller woody species such as Holly, Rowan, Elder or Hazel. Each understorey species will have its own insects. So, each should be examined carefully. You cannot assume, for example, that just because you have found all the species on a Rowan then the Hazel next to it will have nothing new. Always check each plant species in a habitat.

The upper branches of the mature trees form the 'canopy' layer. The canopy of an old oak woodland will be home to a large number of species, often in populations counted in millions, or even billions! Unless you are a bird, however, most of the canopy is out of reach. The spring abundance of caterpillars in the tree canopy provides the food for each new generation of some of our most popular birds, such as Blue Tits and Great Tits. Blue Tits require 40,000 caterpillars to rear a clutch of chicks. The eggs laid all over trees by adult moths will feed birds such as Treecreepers and Long-tailed Tits through the winter months.

The edges of a woodland often provide the most accessible diversity of insects. This does not just mean the outer edges. Edge habitats are formed by rides (wide tracks) through woodland and glades where mature trees have fallen, leaving holes in the canopy. The image here shows a wide-open area in the Wyre Forest, it is particularly rich in species.

Edge habitats often have a better ground flora due to increased light penetration. Also, the branches of the canopy trees come lower down bringing more insects within reach. The lower branches of trees can be swept with a net. However, it is often more productive to beat the branches onto a sheet.

The three main layers of a woodland are just the beginning of the story. A good insect woodland will have countless micro-habitats providing homes for an amazing range of insects. As you get to know your woodland patch, you will notice more and more of these habitats.

Many of the insects found in woodlands can be found in other habitats. Species associated with trees and bushes in parks, gardens and farmland are usually woodland insects that have adapted to survive in less woody habitats. However, the majority of species found in woodlands require specific micro-habitats that can only be provided by extensive old woodlands. Most of these micro-habitats have a fleeting existence and are easily destroyed. Fungi and dead wood habitats are especially vulnerable. The more extensive a woodland is, the easier it is for insects to find a succession of their preferred habitats. Hence, the greatest diversities are found in the largest, oldest woodlands. It is important, though, not to assume insect populations are large and not threatened just because their woodlands are extensive. The micro-habitats they live in will not be extensive and many species will only exist in small numbers. Do not take too many specimens of individual species, you may be inadvertently removing an entire local population.

What follows is only a fraction of the species I have found and recorded in woodland habitats.

The Brimstone butterfly, Gonepteryx rhamni, [30mm FWL] lays eggs on buckthorns which grow in the understorey of woodlands. The adults are often seen in flowery meadows in the summer.

Silver-washed Fritillaries, Argynnis paphia, [35mm FWL] lay eggs on violets growing along woodland rides. The adults can often be seen at brambles in large numbers.

The larvae of Purple-hairstreak butterflies, Favonius quercus, live on the buds and leaves of mature oaks. It is a species that has increased in recent years.

Adult Purple-hairstreaks [16mm FWL] fly mainly in the canopy, but they can sometimes be seen on foliage lower down.

This pupa was found under moss in a woodland. The adult emerged a few weeks later.

The pupa (above) hatched into this Ringet, Aphantopus hyperantus [21mm FWL]. The larvae feed on various grasses while the adults are commonly seen flying around trees.

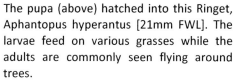

The Yellow Horned moth, Achlya flavicornis, [16mm FWL] flies from February to April in woodlands. It has orange-yellow antennae, hence its name.

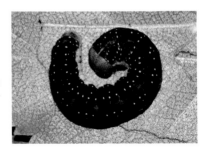

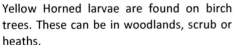

Yellow Horned larvae are found on birch trees. These can be in woodlands, scrub or heaths.

The Beautiful Carpet, Mesoleuca albicillata, [15mm FWL] is a moth of mature woodlands. It can be disturbed from vegetation from June to August.

The larvae of the Beautiful Carpet feed on brambles and Hazel. They over-winter as pupae and are easy to rear in captivity.

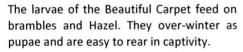

The Wood Carpet, Epirrhoe rivata, [14mm FWL] can be found in open woodland. It often sits with its wings closed like a butterfly.

The Spruce Carpet, Thera britannica, [10mm FWL] has two flight periods. It can be seen in most woodlands with coniferous trees.

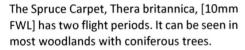

The larvae of the Brindled Pug, Eupithecia abbreviata, [9mm FWL] can be beaten from oaks, sometimes in large numbers. The adults fly from March to May and will come to lights.

The Speckled Yellow, Pseudopanthera macularia, [11mm FWL] can be quite common in daylight along woodland rides where the larvae feed on Wood Sage.

The Scalloped Hazel, Odontopera bidentata, [15mm FWL] can be found in most wooded habitats. The eggs are laid on a variety of tree and shrub species.

The larvae of the Feathered Thorn, Colotois pennaria, feed on the foliage of a variety of woodland trees after spending the winter as eggs.

The adult Feathered Thorn [18mm FWL] flies from September to November. Males are encountered more often than females.

The Clouded Magpie, Abraxas sylvata, [9mm FWL] only flies in woodlands where the larval foodplant, elm, grows.

The Clouded Border, Lomaspilis marginata, [15mm FWL] occurs in wooded areas where poplar and sallow grow. They fly in two broods across most of Britain.

The larvae of the Iron Prominent, Notodonta dromedarius, are found mainly on birch and Alder. They turn browner as they mature.

The adult Iron Prominent [17mm FWL] flies in two broods in most wooded habitats where the larval food plants grow.

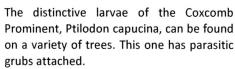

The distinctive larvae of the Coxcomb Prominent, Ptilodon capucina, can be found on a variety of trees. This one has parasitic grubs attached.

The adult Coxcomb Prominent [17mm FWL] can be found in most wooded habitats across Britain.

Larvae of the White Satin, Leucoma salicis, feed on sallow and poplar in damp wooded habitats. It is most common in the Midlands and East Anglia.

Black Arches, Lymantria monacha, [18mm FWL] can be found in mature woodlands during July and August. It will come to moth lights. Their larvae can be beaten from oaks.

The Wood Tiger, Parasemia plantaginis, [15mm FWL] can be seen in a variety of habitats including open woodland.

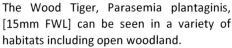

The Red-necked Footman, Atolmis rubricollis, [14mm FWL] can be found in a variety of woodlands. The larvae feed on lichens and algae growing on trees.

The larvae of the Copper Underwing, Amphipyra pyramidea, feed on the foliage of many trees and shrubs.

The adults of the Copper Underwing [20mm FWL] occur in most wooded habitats with a preference for mature woodlands.

Angle Shades, Phlogophora meticulosa, [21mm FWL] can be seen almost anywhere at most times of the year. It can be common in wooded habitats where the wing shape and pattern provide camouflage in leaf litter or on bark.

Dyseriocrania supurpurella [7mm FWL] flies by day and night in woodlands across Britain. The larvae mine the leaves of oaks.

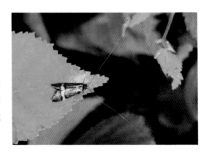

Nemophora degeerella [9mm FWL] is a longhorn moth of the Adelidae family. It can often be seen in large numbers around oak trees in sunshine.

Psyche casta is a bagworm moth of the Psychidae family. Larvae in this family live in cases constructed from debris. The cases of Psyche casta are often seen on tree trunks.

Morophaga choragella [13mm FWL] is a woodland moth. The larvae can be found in bracket fungi. This specimen was reared from larvae in a Ganoderma adspersum bracket.

Coleophora laricella is one of many case-bearing moths. This species lives only on European Larch.

The distinctive case of Coleophora ibipennella can be found on oak leaves. Case-bearers can be reared in captivity or rear them in the wild by netting them on their foodplants.

Diurnea fagella [11mm FWL] is a common woodland moth. The larvae feed between leaves spun together with silk. They use many deciduous tree species.

The Chequered Fruit-tree Tortrix, Pandemis corylana, [10mm FWL] can be found wherever there are trees and shrubs.

Acleris forsskaleana [7mm FWL] can be found around Sycamore and maples in wooded areas. Late instar larvae can be found in rolled leaves.

Lobesia reliquana [6mm FWL] can be found in open woodlands. The larvae feed on oaks, birches and Blackthorn.

Pammene regina [7mm FWL] is common and widespread. The larvae feed on the leaves of Sycamore and maples.

Cydia splendana [9mm FWL] is common in a variety of wooded habitats. The larvae feed in the nuts of oaks, Sweet Chestnut or Walnut.

Ctenophora pecticornis [22mm FWL] is one of several black and yellow craneflies. They are found around woodlands and the larvae live in decaying wood.

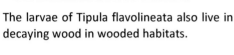

The larvae of Tipula flavolineata also live in decaying wood in wooded habitats.

This adult Tipula flavolineata was reared from the pupa above. It was found in a rotten tree trunk.

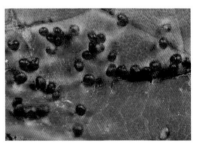

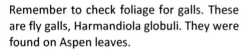

Remember to check foliage for galls. These are fly galls, Harmandiola globuli. They were found on Aspen leaves.

Chironomid flies are commonly beaten from tree foliage or swept from woodland vegetation. This species is Microtendipes pedellus [4mm FWL].

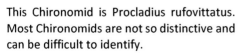

This Chironomid is Procladius rufovittatus. Most Chironomids are not so distinctive and can be difficult to identify.

Rhagio lineola [7mm FWL] is one of a number of similar snipe-flies of the Rhagionidae family. This species is a woodland specialist often seen resting on tree foliage.

Tabanus bromius [11mm FWL] is a horsefly of the Tabanidae family. This species used to be found in many habitats including woodland edge.

This soldier-fly, Sargus bipunctatus, [10mm FWL] appears in the autumn. It can be swept from foliage along the edges of woodlands.

Bombylius major [12mm FWL] is one of several bee-flies. Their larvae are parasites of mining bees. This female is laying eggs along a sandy woodland ride.

A number of hoverflies are bumblebee mimics. Cheilosia illustrata [9mm FWL] is associated with Hogweed along woodland rides and edges.

Criorhina floccosa [12mm FWL] is another bumblebee mimic. It is often seen around the bases of old trees.

158

Chrysotoxum arcuatum [9mm FWL] is one of five very similar species. They can be difficult to identify. This species is more common in coniferous woodlands in the north and west.

Leucozona glaucia [10mm FWL] is an easily identified hoverfly. It can be seen in numbers at Hogweed flowers along woodland rides.

Ferdinandea cuprea [9mm FWL] is another readily identified hoverfly. It is commonly seen basking on foliage or tree trunks in wooded habitats.

Dexiosoma caninum [10mm FWL] is a woodland Tachinid fly. It can be swept from bracken in numbers. The larvae are parasites on the Cockchafer beetle.

Helina depuncta [6mm FWL] is in the Muscidae family, related to houseflies. It can be found by sweeping foliage in woodlands.

Phaonia subventa [7mm FWL] is one of several similar species. It lays eggs in rotting leaves, rotting wood or carrion in wooded habitats. These species need to be caught for accurate identification.

Cychrus caraboides [17mm] can be found under logs or hibernating in dead wood. It eats mainly slugs and snails. This species can stridulate, it makes a squeaking noise when handled.

Notiophilus biguttatus [5.5mm] is the commonest of eight species in the same genus. They are all fast runners and found on the ground under logs and stones.

Loricera pilicornis [7.5mm] prefers woodlands or other shady habitats. It can often be found under logs or dry bark. The pits on the elytra and the bristles on the antennae make it distinctive.

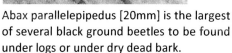

Abax parallelepipedus [20mm] is the largest of several black ground beetles to be found under logs or under dry dead bark.

Badister bullatus [5.5mm] can be found in many habitats. It can often be seen under bark or in tussocks during the winter months, especially along woodland edges or streams.

Anisotoma humeralis [3.7mm] is one of a number of small Leiodid species associated with fungi. This one was found under fungoid bark.

160

Silpha atrata [13mm] is in the carrion beetle family, the Silphidae. It can often be found in numbers under bark or in rotten wood during the winter. The colour varies but the black form is more common.

Rove beetles are well represented in wooded habitats. This Lesteva punctata was found in leaf litter by suction sampling.

This Dropephylla ioptera [2.7mm] was found under bark in a log pile along a track in a coniferous plantation.

Scaphidium quadrimaculatum [5.3mm] is one of the more distinctive rove beetles. It is associated with dead branches infected by fungi.

Atrecus affinis [7mm] is another distinctive rove beetle. It is common under moist bark and in damp rotten wood.

Philonthus decorus [12mm] is one of many similar species. Numbers of them can be found in rotten leaf litter, under logs and bark and in dead wood.

Quedius nigriceps [8.5mm] is one the more distinctive members of its genus. It can be found in litter and moss on woodland floors.

The larvae and adults of Sinodendron cylindricum [15mm] can be found in the fallen trunks of broadleaved trees. It is a relative of the Stag Beetle.

Microcara testacea [5mm] is in the Sciritidae family of marsh beetles. This species can be beaten from foliage or vegetation in marshy areas of woodlands.

Throscid beetles are similar to click beetles. Trixagus dermestoides [2.6mm] can be swept from vegetation in wooded areas.

The larvae of many click beetles live in dead wood. Ampedus balteatus [8.5mm] is one of a number of mainly red species. It is also one of the commonest, though still scarce.

Ampedus sanguinolentus [11mm] is the most distinctive of the 12 Ampedus species. It is a scarce species found mainly in the south and is associated with birches.

162

Platycis minutus [8mm] belongs to the Lycidae or net-winged beetles. They are all associated with dead and rotten wood in woodlands.

Several soldier beetle species are common in wooded habitats. Cantharis decipiens [7mm] can be swept from vegetation or foliage in broadleaved woods.

The adults of Ctesias serra [4.3mm] are not often seen. The hairy larvae, however, are more frequently recorded. They can be found under bark, including the flakes of Sycamore bark, where they steal food from spiders.

Ptinomorphus imperialis [4.5mm] belongs to the large Ptinidae family. It is a scarce species but can be found on dead wood or nearby foliage in many wooded habitats.

Thymalus limbatus [6mm] is a scarce beetle with a local distribution. It is found under bark infected by fungi in old woodlands.

Soronia grisea [4.6mm] is one of three species in a genus associated with tree sap. They can be seen at sap runs where trees are exuding sap or under sappy bark.

Uleiota planatus [5mm] is in the Silvanidae family. It is an introduced species appearing in Britain in the 19th Century. It has spread across much of England and Wales where it is found under the bark of recently dead trees.

Silvanus bidentatus [3mm] is another introduced Silvanid species. Mainly found under the bark of broadleaved trees, it remains local and scarce.

Rhizophagus ferrugineus [3.6mm] is one of thirteen similar species. All are associated with sap and fungoid bark in wooded habitats.

Trees are usually covered with aphids that attract a number of ladybird species. The Orange Ladybird, Halyzia sedecimguttata, [5.3mm] can be beaten from trees and will come to lights.

The Latridiidae, or mould beetle family, has many small species that can be sieved from leaf litter. Stephostethus lardarius is less than 3mm long.

Enicmus brevicornis, also in the Latridiidae, can be found under bark with powdery fungi. This species is 2mm or less.

Orchesia undulata [4.5mm] is in the Melandryidae family. It can be found in decaying wood across most of Britain, but it is not common.

Pycnomerus fuliginosus [4.8mm] has been introduced from Australia. It is found under bark and is spreading across Britain.

Corticeus unicolor [6mm] is a Tenebrid species found under bark. This species is a predator of bark beetles.

Oudemera femoralis [17mm] is a scarce species usually found in wooded areas. It can be swept from Ivy or sallow flowers.

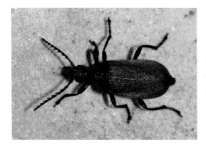

Pyrochroa serraticornis [12mm] larvae are often seen under fungoid bark. It is one of three 'cardinal beetles' in the Pyrochroidae family.

Vincenzellus ruficollis [3mm] is one of several similar species in the Salpingidae family. They are found under bark across most of Britain, but they are scarce.

There are seventy longhorn beetle species in Britain. Most are associated with wooded habitats. Rhagium bifasciatum [16mm] is found around coniferous trees including plantations.

Most longhorn larvae live in wood, living or dead. They can be reared in captivity with varying success. This one is Rhagium mordax.

Paracorymbia fulva [12mm] is a rare longhorn. It can be found visiting flowers in woodlands.

Pachytodes cerambyciformis [8mm] can also be found on flowers, especially umbellifers such as Hogweed.

Pyrrhidium sanguineum [11mm] has been spreading in recent years. It is more likely to be beaten from the foliage of trees or vegetation.

Anaglyptus mysticus [10mm] is widespread in England and Wales. The larvae take two years to develop. This is the case with many longhorn species due to the poor nutritional quality of their food.

166

A number of leaf beetles from the Chrysomelidae family are found in woodlands. The adults of Clytra quadripunctata [9mm] can be beaten from trees. Their larvae live in ant nests feeding on plant material and ant poo.

Many leaf beetles can be swept from herbage along woodland rides. Chrysolina staphylaea [7.3mm] feeds on a number of plants including buttercups and plantains.

Phyllobrotica quadrimaculata [6.5mm] feeds on skullcaps in a variety of habitats. This one was swept from herbage in an area of wet woodlands.

Tortoise beetles of the Cassidinae can be swept from herbage along woodland rides. Cassida murraea [7.5mm] starts off green but turns red as it matures.

Weevils are common in wooded habitats. Attelabus nitens [5mm] lays eggs in rolled leaves on oaks or Sweet Chestnut.

The Curculio genus has six species that feed on the catkins and nuts of various trees. Curculio glandium [5.4mm] can be beaten from oaks.

The Cionus genus has six species that feed mainly on figworts. This one is Cionus scrophulariae [4.3mm]. They can be common along woodland rides where their foodplants grow.

The larvae of Hylobius abietis [11mm] create galleries as they feed under the bark of conifers. The adults can be beaten from trees or swept from vegetation.

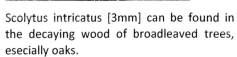

Dryocoetes villosus [3mm] is one of many cylindrical bark beetles in the Scolytinae subfamily. It is found in the bark of oaks.

Scolytus intricatus [3mm] can be found in the decaying wood of broadleaved trees, esecially oaks.

Trypodendron signatum [3.7mm] is found in the dead wood of broadleaved trees in ancient woodlands.

Platypus cylindrus [5.3mm] is a pin-hole borer of the Platypodinae subfamily. Males bore holes deep into the trees, then females lay eggs in the galleries.

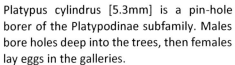

Numerous rove beetle species are asscoiated with fungi. Many of them are small and hard to identify. Quedius truncicola [11mm] is larger and more distinctive. It can be found in rot holes with fungi.

Pocadius adustus [3.4mm] is one of two related sap beetles. It can be found in puffball fungi of the Lycoperdon genus.

Glischrochilus quadriguttatus [4.7mm] is a sap beetle. It is associated with sap runs but can also be found in rotting fungi.

Cryptophagus lycoperdi [2.9mm] is one of many silken fungus beetles. This species can be found on earthball fungi of the Scleroderma genus.

Triplax aenea [3.8mm] is one the pleasing fungus beetle of the Erotylidae family. It is found in fungi on old trees.

Bipyhllus lunatus [3.3mm] is associated with the Crampball fungi, Daldinia concentrica, on dead ash trees.

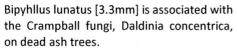

Mycetophagus multipunctatus [4.4mm] is one of seven species in a genus of hairy fungus beetles. It can be found in bracket fungi, especially Chicken-of-the-Woods.

Cis bidentatus [2.4mm] is one of a number of small beetles in the Ciidae family associated with fungi. They can be hard to identify.

Hallomenus binotatus [4.8mm] is a rare species in the Tetratomidae family. It is found in bracket fungi.

Eledona agricola [3.3mm] is found in Chicken-of-the-Woods fungi. Look for them in fungi that has become dry and powdery.

Diaperis boleti [7.3mm] is found mainly in the South East. Look for specimens in old and decaying bracket fungi.

Platyrhinus resinosus [10mm] is one of several fungus weevils in the Anthribidae family. Find them on Ash trees with crampball fungi.

Bumblebee queens are often found hibernating under bark in woodlands. This one is the Tree Bumblebee, Bombus hypnorum [12mm FWL]. If you find them, leave them covered up where they are.

Predatory wasps, such as this Mellinus arvensis, [10mm] can be swept from foliage along woodland rides.

Wood Ants, Formica rufa, [10mm] build large nest mounds from debris on the woodland floor. They prefer conifer forests.

The females of Odynerus spinipes [10mm] make paper nests underground. This specimen was seen in a woodland clearing.

Wasp galls form on herbage as well as trees. The galls of Liposthenes glechomae are found on Ground Ivy which often grows along woodland rides and edges.

Neuroterus quercusbaccarum causes disc-shaped galls on oak leaves. There are several similar types of galls found on oaks.

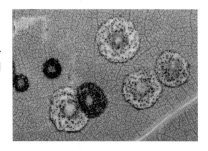

Numerous parasitic wasps take advantage of the insect diversity in woodlands. Barylypa propugnator uses the larvae of moths. This specimen was seen along a woodland edge.

The female Glypta fronticornis has a very long ovipositor. It belongs to the Banchinae subfamily.

Many parasitic species, such as this Collyria trichophthalma, [7mm] can be found at woodland edges reflecting the higher diversity of host species.

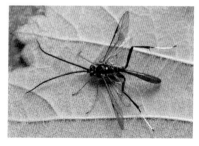

Members of the Cryptinae subfmily can be difficult to identify. This is a male Cryptus armator.

Most parasitic wasp species are greatly under recorded. There are just nine records of Exephanes ischioxanthus [10mm] on NBN Atlas.

Females of the Ichneumon genus can be found hibernating under bark and moss in woodlands. This Ichneumon gracilentus [11mm] was in the damp wood of a rotten Beech trunk.

Numerous sawfly species lay eggs on the foliage of trees. The large larvae of Cimbex femorata can be found on birches. They can be reared in captivity to obtain adults.

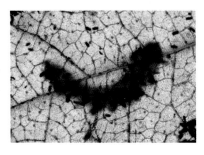

Some sawfly larvae are leaf-miners. Many of them, such as this Scolioneura betuleti, can be identified from their mines.

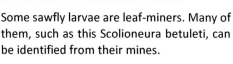

The Willow Sawfly, Nematus oligospilus, [6mm] can be found around willows including those growing along woodland edges and rides.

Dolerus triplicatus [10mm] lays eggs on Juncus rushes. They can be found wherever their foodplants grow, including wet areas in woodlands.

Tenthredo livida [14mm] can be beaten from foliage along woodland rides. The larvae feed at night on a variety of trees.

The distinctive Figwort Sawfly, Tenthredo scrophulariae, [13mm] lays eggs on figworts along woodland rides or other places where the foodplants grow.

A number of bug species can be found hibernating under bark. Flatbugs of the Araidae family, such as Aneurus avenius [4.5mm], live under bark all year round.

Ground vegetation in woodlands is home to many bug species. Rhopalus subrufus [7.3mm] can be swept from herbage in clearings.

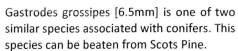

Leaf litter in woodlands is home to ground bugs. Drymus brunneus [4.5mm] is a common species found by seiving litter.

Gastrodes grossipes [6.5mm] is one of two similar species associated with conifers. This species can be beaten from Scots Pine.

Empicoris vagabundus [6.5mm] is one of several thread-legged bugs. It can be found around trees and shrubs in wooded areas.

Pantilius tunicatus [9mm] can be beaten from the lower branches of several tree species, including Hazel and Alder.

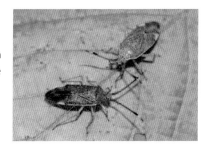

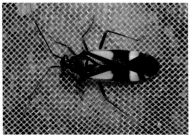

Dryophilocoris flavoquadrimaculatus is one of many Mirid bugs that can be found on trees. This species is common on oaks in May and June.

Iassus lanio [7.4mm] is a large leafhopper commonly found on oaks. It varies from green to brown

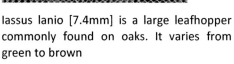

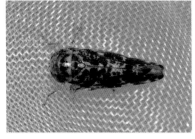

Adult Allygus mixtus [6.5mm] can be beaten from many woodland trees. Their nymphs feed on grasses.

Aphids are common in woodlands, not just on the trees. Brachycaudus lychnidis can be swept from Red Campion growing along rides.

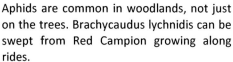

Macrosiphum rosae [2.5mm] can be found infesting Dog Rose along rides and woodland edges.

Psyllopsis fraxini [3.5mm] feed on ash trees. There are three species that are indistinguishable. They all cause galls in the form of rolled leaf edges.

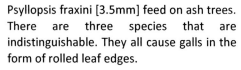

Various species of springtails are common in woodland habitats. This Monobella grassei [1.6mm] was found under the bark of a fallen Beech tree.

Protaphorura aurantiaca [2.5mm] is one of many species that can be seived from leaf litter.

Allacma fusca [3.5mm] is a globular springtail that can be swept from hearbage along woodland rides.

Ectobius pallidus [8mm] is one of our native cockroaches. This one was found in a pile of dead branches in open woodland.

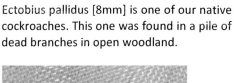

Barkfly species are common around trees. This Mesopsocus unipunctatus [5mm] was beaten from oak foliage.

Thrips are more often seen in flowers, however, some are asscociated with dead plant material and fungi. This Hoplothrips fungi was beaten from bracken in a woodland.

Water and Wetland Safaris

Water based habitats come in many different forms, each with their own challenges for wildlife. This means that different types of wetland habitats have different ranges of insects. Most of us have some type of wetland habitat nearby. This can be anything from a local pond to a lake, a major river or even the coast.

The most obvious water-based habitats are those with open water. These range from small ponds to large lakes, rivers and streams. The open water of large lakes and reservoirs are of least interest to entomologists. There are not many insects that can tolerate cold, deep water. So, you do not need to buy a boat! Some insects, such as stoneflies and mayflies have aquatic larvae that live on the stony beds of faster flowing rivers and streams where the oxygen levels are high.

We have a good range of beetles and bugs that live, at least partly, aquatic lives. Most of them prefer to live in still or slow-moving waters. They usually require plenty of aquatic vegetation or nutrient rich silts where vegetation has rotted on the water's bottom. Such waters are usually full of microscopic life which forms the basis of the food web. This includes algae and micro-organisms such as water fleas.

As with woodland, the largest variety of insects will usually be found in the edge habitats. These habitats are both in and out of the water. In the water look for areas with emergent vegetation. This is made up of plants growing up out of the water. The most obvious ones being Bulrushes, Reeds and Yellow Flag Iris. Here you need to pond dip for beetles and bugs living among the submerged plant stems. Either tip the contents of your net into a plastic tray or pot individual specimens straight from the net. Different water bodies will often have a different range of species. This means trying everything from overgrown drainage ditches and canals to the edges of lakes and rivers.

Many small aquatic species prefer to live in mats of pond weed or algae or even in the rotting debris on the bottom of the water. These habitats can be messy and smelly, but it is usually worth the effort. Use a net to scoop up samples and tip into a tray for closer examination. Try teasing apart mats of weeds and algae. Then wait a few minutes for insects to stir and show themselves.

Do not forget the parts of the plants above the water. These can be swept for a variety of insects. Also, try looking between the leaves and stems of taller water plants. Bulrushes are particularly good targets for this type of search. Just tease back a few leaves to reveal hidden beetles and bugs that are not easily obtained by sweeping.

Consider the land around a water body as an edge habitat. In these places will grow plants that prefer to have wet feet but do not like to be permanently standing in the water. This includes plants such as sedges, rushes and Meadowsweet. There are likely to be wetland trees such as willows and Alder too.

The low vegetation (herbage) should be swept or beaten directly into a tray. There is usually a good variety of species in these wet edge habitats. Many of the insects found here will not be found in drier places. Use a beating tray to obtain species from the trees. Willows, in particular, have many associated insect species.

This is a man-made flood pond, it was about four years old when the photo was taken. It shows edge habitats both in and out of the water. There are various water plants growing around the shallow edges and water lilies growing in the middle. The vegetated banks and even the bare muddy bank on the right are viable micro-habitats.

Larger wetland complexes often have a mix of open water and drainage channels. Drainage channels are often richer in insects than the ponds and lakes they drain, mainly because there are fewer fish. This image shows a drainage channel at Doxey Marshes in Staffordshire. It is rich in insect life. When working around habitats like this be mindful of birds nesting in the vegetation during the spring months.

Meadows next to lakes are often flooded for part of the year. This image shows a meadow at Aqualate Mere NNR in Staffordshire. There is a good mix of plant life ranging from grasses to trees. The edge of the meadow runs into a reedbed that extends out into the lake. Places like this usually have a rich variety of insect species.

The vegetation in wet meadows can be tall and quite tough. Many insects will be missed if you only use a sweep net. The way to find more insects in this habitat is to shake the vegetation over a beating tray. If the meadow is dry enough, you could try using a suction sampler. This will pick up species running on the ground and hiding in the leaf litter.

The natural habitat of a number of insect species, especially beetles and ground bugs, is riverine gravels. These gravel banks form in rivers and are usually exposed when the waters are low. We do not have much of this habitat due to over-management of our rivers. This image shows a section of the River Trent in Staffordshire.

In recent decades numerous shallow sand and gravel quarries have appeared along a number of our river systems. When these quarries are abandoned they become havens for wildlife. Many have gravelly banks that resemble riverine habitats. This one is not far away from the image shown above. It has a rich beetle fauna. Quarries should always be searched with care. They are dangerous places.

Many wetland habitats do not have a lot of open water. Sometimes they are not obviously wetlands. The moorlands of upland Britain are often quite wet. Within these places there will be areas that are very wet, all year round. There will usually be some open water in the form of small peaty pools and streams. Such areas are often dominated by sedges and rushes. The vegetation can be swept or beaten into a tray. Or handfuls of plant material can be sieved into a tray and teased apart. Try using a suction sampler if it is not too wet. Along the streams look under overhanging areas and under rocks. Also, keep an eye open for damselflies and dragonflies.

Peat bogs are a wet habitat, they are formed by mosses that hold on to the water, often acidifying it. It can feel like walking on a giant sponge. These are specialised habitats for specialised insects. These habitats are often dominated by mosses and cotton grasses. This image shows part of the Whixall Moss NNR complex in Shropshire.

There are a number of floating bogs in Britain, such as Chartley Moss NNR. These places look like ordinary peat bogs, but they have lakes under the peat. They are special places, and most are protected. They are also very dangerous!

Where the land along a river flattens out into wide expanses you may find flood meadows. These are areas that experience floods on a regular basis but are not usually under water for long periods. The silt from the flood water enriches the soils allowing the vegetation to grow lush. Sadly, most of these places are intensively farmed. Where the farming pressure is reduced, there can be a wide variety of natural vegetation and associated insects. After heavy rains there are often piles of debris that settle in flood plains along our larger rivers. These litter piles can be sieved for beetles and bugs that have washed down the rivers. Many of the species found this way are otherwise rarely seen.

As with hedgerows many of the ponds found in farmland have been lost. Most were filled in and drainage installed to stop them reforming. This meant the loss of the aquatic habitat and the surrounding wetland trees and herbage that provided refuge for many insect species.

However, some areas still have a good number of ponds. You may find that they are ploughed right up to the edge and any trees have been grubbed out, but they still provide a wet habitat. If there are trees or herbage try the usual beating and netting. Then get your net wet, go for some dipping. There are likely to be a few species of beetles and bugs, including weevils that live on pondweeds. Some weevils actually live under the water, these need to be looked for carefully by teasing apart pondweeds in a tray. Sadly, I am still looking. These species are not at all common.

What follows is a selection of species I have found and recorded in a variety of wetland habitats.

Not many of our Lepidoptera are restricted to wetlands. The Green-veined White, Pieris napi, [20mm FWL] can occur in many habitats. It is often common in wetlands where it feeds on Cuckooflower.

Likewise, the Marsh Fritillary, Euphydryas aurinia, [19mm FWL] occurs in many habitats but is more commonly seen in wet areas. It has declined greatly in recent times.

The Drinker, Euthrix potatoria, [25mm FWL] prefers damp grasslands and reed beds. The larvae are known to drink water droplets from blades of grass.

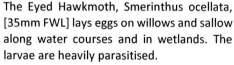

The Eyed Hawkmoth, Smerinthus ocellata, [35mm FWL] lays eggs on willows and sallow along water courses and in wetlands. The larvae are heavily parasitised.

Alder Moths, Acronicta alni, lay eggs on several tree species. They often use Alder in wet habitats.

The young larvae of Alder Moths look like bird droppings (above). Later instars are black and yellow (right).

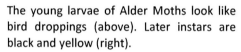

The Light Knot Grass, Acronicta menyanthidis, [16mm FWL] can be found in wetlands, moorlands and peat bogs. Larvae can be swept from Heather, Bilberry and Bog Myrtle.

The Brown-veined Wainscot, Archanara dissoluta, [12mm FWL] is found in reed beds. There are many similar wainscot moths in wetlands.

The Small Clouded Brindle, Apamea unanimis, [15mm FWL] is found in a variety of wet habitats. The larvae feed on wetland grasses.

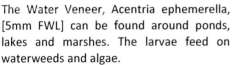

The Water Veneer, Acentria ephemerella, [5mm FWL] can be found around ponds, lakes and marshes. The larvae feed on waterweeds and algae.

The Ringed China-mark, Parapoynx stratiotata, [9mm FWL] can be found around most open water habitats including canals and ditches.

The Beautiful China-mark, Nymphula nitidulata, [8mm FWL] is found along rivers and streams and in fens and marshes. Larvae feed on Bur-reed and Yellow Waterlily.

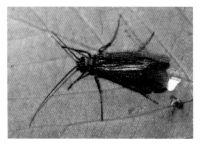

Caddisflies, Trichoptera, are thought to be related to the Lepidoptera. Most have aquatic larvae. Micropterna sequax [16mm] breeds in temporary streams.

Limnephilus vittatus [10mm] is a common species. It is found in pools and reservoirs with bare sandy bottoms. The larvae live in cases made from silk and sand grains.

Glyphotaelius pellucidus [14mm] lives in still waters. The larvae live in the shallow margins and make cases from bits of dead leaves.

Mystacides azurea [8mm] can be seen swarming over streams, rivers and canals. Most caddis larvae are omnivores.

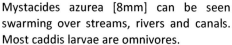

The Bog Bush Cricket, Metrioptera brachyptera, [16mm] can be found in a variety of open habitats including wet areas of moorlands.

The Short-winged Conehead, Conocephalus dorsalis, [14mm] can be found in salt marshes, reed beds and bogs. It is a species that is increasing its range northwards.

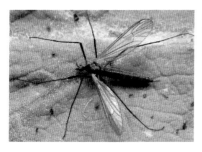

A number of cranefly species are common in wet habitats. This Tricyphona immaculata [8mm FWL] was netted in a well vegetated flood meadow.

Gall causers can be found on wetland vegetation. These galls are caused by the fly Dasineura ulmaria on Meadowsweet.

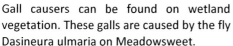

There are about 30 species of mosquitoes in Britain. They all breed in water. This Ochlerotatus rusticus was swept from herbage in a permanently wet woodland.

Crysops relictus [11mm FWL] is sometimes called the Twin-lobed Deerfly. It is found in wet meadows and has a nasty bite.

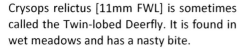

The Four-barred Major, Oxycera rara, [6mm FWL] is one of several similar species found in wetlands and marshes and around the edges of open water.

The Common Green Colonel, Oplodontha viridula, [7mm FWL] is found in wetland habitats. It can often be swept from reeds and has aquatic larvae.

Empis tessellata [11mm FWL] can be found in open habitats including lush wet grasslands. Adults can often be seen hunting on umbellifers. The male has to present a dead insect as a gift before a female will mate.

The hoverfly Anasimyia lineata [7mm FWL] is found in emergent vegetation around the edges of still and slow moving water. It is often seen around Bulrushes.

The bumble-bee mimic, Eristalis intricaria, [10mm FWL] prefers damp habitats such as wet meadows. It can be seen visiting blue and purple flowers such as knapweeds.

Loxocera albiseta is one of several similar species that need to be examined in hand for identification. This one is found where rushes grow in wet habitats.

The picture-winged fly Rivellia syngenesiae is found is marshes and damp places. The larvae feed on Greater Bird's-foot Trefoil.

Sepedon sphegea [9mm FWL] has larvae that feed on aquatic snails. It can be found in many wet habitats from flood meadows to the edges of vegetated lakes.

Gyrinus substriatus [6mm] is the commonest of 12 whirligig beetles in the Gyrinidae family. This species can be seen in large numbers swarming on the water surface. Most species require dissection for identification.

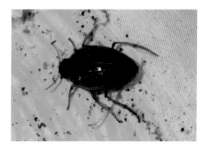

Haliplus ruficollis [2.7mm] is one of 19 crawling water beetles. They are found in vegetated water and can easily slip through small holes in a net.

The Screech Beetle, Hygrobia hermanni, [9.3mm] can be found in ponds, lakes or slow-moving waters. They will often screech when handled.

Agabus didymus [7.8mm] can be found in vegetated streams, ditches or bog pools. This one was found in a ditch running through sand dunes.

Colymbetes fuscus [16mm] is a large water beetle. It is found in ponds and ditches across Britain. This species occasionally comes to light.

Acilius sulcatus [17mm] is a scarce species. It prefers waters with no fish. The female (shown) has grooves running along the elytra. The male's elytra are smooth.

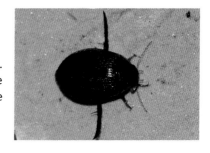

The genus Dysticus contains 6 of our largest diving beetles. Dysticus semisulcatus [26mm] is a scarce species preferring acidic waters. This one was found in a peat bog pool.

Nebrioporus elegans [4.7mm] is one of 4 related small diving beetles. This one was found in an old quarry lake.

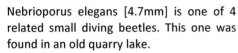

Hygrotus impressopunctatus [4.3mm] was netted with the specimen above. It is a scarce species. Hygrotus is a genus of 9 small diving beetles.

This Hygrotus versicolor [3.4mm] was also found in a disused quarry. It is a more frequently found species.

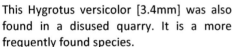

Hyphydrus ovatus [4.6mm] can be found in ponds, ditches and slow moving water. It is common and often found in large numbers.

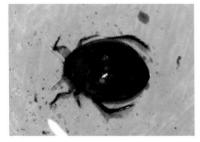

Laccophilus minutus [4.5mm] is one of 3 related species. This one can be found in most watery habitats. They are very active when caught in a net.

Elaphrus cupreus [9mm] can be found by fresh water. They like to run along the ground in short bursts and to bask on vegetation in sunshine.

Bembidion dentellum [5.5mm] is one of a number of species in the genus found near water. This one prefers vegetated marshes.

Oxypselaphus obscurus [5.8mm] can be seived from litter in marshes and wet woodlands. This one was found in a wooded peat bog.

Amara apricaria [7.5mm] can be found under stones on disturbed soils such as the vegetated edges and sand and gravel pits.

Chlaenius vestitus [10mm] is one of 4 similar species. This one was found in shingle beds at the edge of a lake in an old quarry.

Demetrias monostigma [5mm] can be found in reed and sedge litter. It will also hide in the stems of Bulrush. There are 2 other species in the genus.

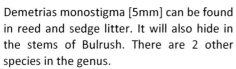

Helochares punctatus [5.5mm] prefers peaty acidic pools on moors. This one was found in a peat bog drain. There are 3 species in the genus.

Ochthebius minimus [1.75mm] is one of 14 similar moss beetles. This one was found in algal mats pulled from a pond.

Bryoporus cernuus is a rarley recorded rove beetle. This one was found by suction sampler in a semi-permanent wet medow.

Hygronoma dimidata [2.75mm] is a small rove beetle that is usually found in reed beds. Try looking for them in reed stems during winter.

Dianous coerulescens [7mm] is associated with mossy stones by streams. This one was found in wet moss and litter on a small waterfall.

Species of the family Dryopidae are known as long-toed water beetles. Dryops luridus [4mm] can be found in mud or under stones by water. This one was found under a stone by a moorland stream.

Most of our click beetles are not closely assocaiated with water. Actenicerus sjaelandicus [13mm] is an exception, it prefers damp habitats. This one was swept from vegetation in a peat bog.

Cantharis cryptica [7.5mm] is a soldier beetle that can be swept from vegetation in marshes and wet grasslands.

Anthocomus rufus [4.5mm] prefers damp meadows and fens. Where it occurs, it can be found in large numbers.

Kateretes pusillus [2.75mm] is one of 3 species that live on sedges and rushes in marshy places. Numbers of these were swept from herbage in a wet meadow.

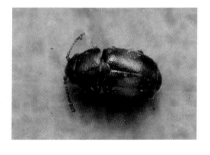

Psammoecus bipunctatus [2.6mm] is found in fens and marshes. During the winter they can be found in the stems of reeds and Bulrushes.

The Water Ladybird, Anisosticta novemdecimpunctata, [3.5mm] lives in most wetlands. It can be swept from waterside plants during the summer or seived from tussocks in the winter.

Leptura quadrifasciata [15mm] is a scarce longhorn beetle. As with most longhorns they are associated with trees but this species is usually found in wet places. This one was spotted on a fence at Aqualate Mere NNR.

There are 15 species of leaf beetles in the genus Donacia. Donacia crassipes [10mm] is found around waterlilies in open water such lakes and ponds.

Chrysolina polita [7mm] is most often associated with mints. It can be quite common in wet places where Water Mint grows.

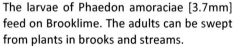

The larvae of Phaedon amoraciae [3.7mm] feed on Brooklime. The adults can be swept from plants in brooks and streams.

Galerucella calmariensis [4.5mm] is one of 6 related species. This one can be found in wetlands where Purple Loosestrife grows.

The 14 species of the genus Dorytomus are associated with poplars and willows. Dorytomus melanophthalmus [3.5mm] can be beaten from willows in wetlands.

The Beautiful Demoiselle, Calopteryx virgo, [40mm] prefers fast flowing waters with sandy or pebbly bottoms. It is more common in Wales and the south west of England but can be found elsewhere.

The Emerald Damsefly, Lestes sponsa, [30mm] prefers acidic bogs and waters with lush emergent vegetation.

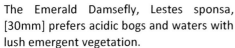

The Large Red Damselfly, Pyrrhosoma nymphula, [28mm] can be found around ponds, canals and ditches. It is a common species.

The Migrant Hawker, Aeshna mixta, [45mm] breeds in gravel pits, lakes and ponds. This species has increased in numbers and range.

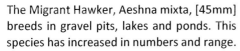

The Broad-bodied Chaser, Libellula depressa, [26mm] occurs in most open water habitats, including garden ponds. This is an immature male, it will turn powdery blue.

The White-faced Darter, Leucorrhinia dubia, [25mm] is one of our rarest species. It only occurs on bogs with sphagnum mosses. This female is laying eggs. The larvae live among waterlogged mosses for 2 years.

192

The abundance and variety of insects in wetlands attracts a good number of parasites. Proctotrupes gravidator [5mm FWL] parasitises the larvae of Amara species of ground beetles. This one was found in a wet meadow.

Several of these Zele deceptor were swept from vegetation on a peat bog. They parasitise mainly Geometrid moth larvae.

Glypta monoceros is one of many species in the same genus. Some can be hard to identify, though there is a modern key. This was swept from herbage in a wet meadow.

Gambrus carnifex [11mm] parasitises arange of moths. This one was swept from umbellifer flowers in a wetland area.

Gelis aerator is one of many species in the genus. Some species are wingless. They often parasitise the cocoons of other parasites. This one was netted on a floating bog.

Diphyus quadripunctorius [15mm] is a large Ichneumonid. It can be swept from vegetation in lush wet meadows.

Many species of sawfly live on wetland vegetation. The larvae of Allantus calceatus feed on the foliage of Meadowsweet. They can be reared in captivity.

Nematus alniastri is one of a number of species to be found on Alder. The larvae of some species will be hiden in rolled or folded leaves.

The larvae of Euura bergmanni feed on willows and sallows. They always feed along the leaf edges with the stripe facing outwards.

Tenthredopsis litterata [10mm] lays eggs on grasses. Adults of this genus are variable in colour making identification more difficult.

Tenthredo arcuata [10mm] lays eggs on clovers. This is one of a group of species where the males are almost indistiguishable. This specimen is a female.

Tenthredo colon [11mm] is one of 5 species with white antennal bands. In wetlands it is associated with Great Willowherb as well as willows and sallows.

The Blue Shieldbug, Zicrona caerulea, [6mm] can be common in wet grasslands. It is a predatory species with a taste for leaf beetles.

Chilacis typhae [4.5mm] is associated with Greater Reedmace and is often called the Bulrush Bug.

The European Chinchbug, Ischnodemus sabuleti, [5.5mm] can be found around reeds and other wetland grasses. The nymphs are red and black.

Coranus subapterus [10.5mm] is an assassin bug predating on other insects. This one was found on a peat bog.

The Marsh damsel Bug, Nabis limbatus, [8.5mm] can be swept from vegetation in wet meadows across Britain.

Chartoscirta cincta [4mm] is a ground dwelling bug. It can be found in litter in marshes or by the edges of open water bodies. Try finding by suction sampler.

The Little Pond Skater, Gerris argentatus, [8mm] is our smallest pond skater. As with other Gerris species it is found skating on the water surface. This one was seen in a bog pool.

The Water Scopion, Nepa cinerea, [20mm] is unmistakeable. Look for it in mats of vegetation in clean ponds.

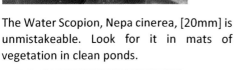

The Water Stick Insect, Ranatra linearis, [40mm] is another unmistakeable water bug. It can also be found in well vegetated ponds. They are easy to miss!

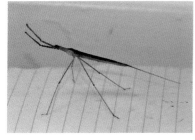

The Saucer Bug, Ilyocoris cimicoides, [15mm] can often be dredged out of mud and algae on the bottom of ponds.

Plea minutissima [2.5mm] is one of our smallest water bugs. It can be found around water plants such as milfoils and crowfoots. It is found in ponds or slow rivers.

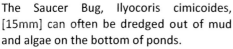

Aphids can be found on wetland vegetation. Tuberolachnus salignus [6mm] is one of our largest aphids. It can be found on willows and sallows. It is possibly widespread but seriously under-recorded.

There are around 50 species of mayflies in Britain, all associated with water. Baetis rhodani is one of the commonest and found along most streams and river systems.

There are over 30 species of stonefly in Britain. All species have aquatic larvae and all are difficult to identify. This one is Isoperla grammatica [12mm FWL].

There are just 3 species of alderflies in Britain. They are usually found near water. They all require examination of genitalia for identification. This one is Sialis lutaria.

A number of springtails are associated with wet habitats. Podura aquatica [2mm] can be found on the surface along the margins of ponds and lakes.

Isotomurus plumosus [2.5mm] is a scarce species but can be found in wetlands across much of Britain.

The tiny Sminthurides aquaticus [0.5mm] is a common species found on the surface of ponds, often clinging to debris.

Index of Species

Paranchus albipes	43	Tachyporus obtusus	75
Patrobus atrorufus	71	Tasgius ater	75
Phaedon amoraciae	190	Tatianaerhynchites aequatus	78
Phillopedon plagiatum	18	Tenebrio molitor	77
Philonthus decorus	160	Tetrops praeustus	79
Philonthus marginatus	139	Thymalus limbatus	162
Phloeonomus punctipennis	117	Timarcha tenebricosa	137
Phylan gibbus	136	Triplax aenea	168
Phyllobrotica quadrimaculata	166	Trixagus dermestoides	161
Pissodes castaneus	138	Trox scaber	116
Platycis minutus	162	Trypodendron signatum	167
Platydracus stercorarius	116	Typhaeus typhoeus	140
Platypus cylindrus	167	Tytthaspis sedecimpunctata	78
Platyrhinus resinosus	169	Uleiota planatus	163
Pocadius adustus	168	Vincenzellus ruficollis	164
Poecilium alni	79		
Poecilus cupreus	71	**Collembola**	
Pogoncherus hispidus	79	Allacma fusca	175
Pogonus chalceus	132	Dicyrtomina saundersi	119
Propylea quattuordecimpunctata	78	Isotomurus plumosus	196
Psammoecus bipunctatus	189	Monobella grassei	175
Psilothrix viridicoerulea	135	Orchesella cincta	10
Ptinomorphus imperialis	162	Podura aquatica	196
Ptomaphagus subvillosus	37	Protaphorura aurantiaca	175
Pycnomerus fuliginosus	164	Seira domestica	87
Pyrochroa serraticornis	164	Sminthurides aquaticus	196
Pyrochroa serraticornis (larva)	15		
Pyrrhidium sanguineum	165	**Dermaptera**	
Quedius nigriceps	161	Forficula auricularia	87
Quedius truncicola	168	Labia minor	87
Rhagium bifasciatum	165		
Rhagium mordax (larva)	165	**Dictyoptera**	
Rhagonycha fulva	76	Ectobius pallidus	175
Rhizophagus ferrugineus	163		
Rhodaphodius foetens	140	**Diptera**	
Rugilus orbiculatus	75	Acrosathe annulata	129
Scaphidium quadrimaculatum	160	Anasimyia lineata	184
Scolytus intricatus	167	Anomoia purmunda	110
Selatosomus aeneus	135	Bibio pomonae	129
Sepedophilus littoreus	75	Bombylius major	157
Sermylassa halensis	137	Calliphora vomitoria	68
Silpha atrata	160	Campiglossa malaris	6
Silpha laevigata	133	Cheilosia albitarsis	6
Silvanus bidentatus	163	Cheilosia illustrata	157
Sinodendron cylindricum	161	Chironomus dorsalis	70
Soronia grisea	162	Chironomus plumosus	70
Sphaeridium scarabaeoides	139	Chloromyia formosa	68
Stenocorus meridianus	7	Chrysotoxum arcuatum	158
Stephostethus lardarius	163	Chrysotoxum bicinctum	130
Tachinus laticollis	139	Chrysotoxum elegans	130
Tachyporus hypnorum	115	Chyrsops viduatus	6

Craneiobia corni (galls)	129	Tachina fera	68
Criorhina floccosa	157	Thereva nobilitata	109
Crysops relictus	183	Tipula fascipennis	109
Ctenophora pecticornis	156	Tipula flavolineata	156
Dasineura tympani (galls)	69	Tipula flavolineata (pupa)	156
Dasineura ulmaria	183	Tipula rufina	69
Dasysyrphus albostriatus	40	Tipula staegeri	69
Dexiosoma caninum	158	Tipula vernalis	6
Dysmachus trigonus	129	Tricyphona immaculata	183
Empis tessellata	184	Urophora jaceana	130
Episyrphus balteatus	67	Volucella inanis	67
Eristalis intricaria	184		
Eristalis tenax	67	**Ephemeroptera**	
Eupeodes luniger	67	Baetis rhodani	196
Ferdinandea cuprea	158	Cloeon dipterum	100
Gymnosoma rotundatum	130	Ephemera danica	10
Haematopota crassicornis	109		
Harmandiola globuli (galls)	156	**Hemiptera**	
Helina depuncta	158	Acanthosoma haemorrhoidale	85
Hydromya dorsalis	110	A. haemorrhoidale (nymph)	85
Leptogaster cylindrica	129	Aelia acuminata	118
Leucozona glaucia	158	Allygus mixtus	174
Leucozona leucorum	109	Alydus calcaratus	143
Loxocera albiseta	184	Aneurus avenius	173
Merzomyia westermannia	130	Aradus depressus	118
Mesembrina meridiana	110	Berytinus minor	144
Microchrysa polita	68	Brachycaudus lychnidis	174
Microtendipes pedellus	156	Centrotus cornutus	9
Musca autumnalis	68	Ceruraphis eriophori	119
Myathropa florea	110	Chartoscirta cincta	194
Nephrotoma appendiculata	109	Chilacis typhae	194
Nephrotoma flavescens	109	Cinara pinea	144
Nephrotoma quadrifaria	69	Coranus subapterus	194
Neria cibaria	6	Coreus marginatus	85
Ochlerotatus rusticus	183	Corizus hyoscyami	9
Oplodontha viridula	183	Daraeocoris ruber	86
Oxycera rara	183	Drepanosiphum platanoidis	86
Phaonia subventa	158	Drymus brunneus	173
Phasia hemiptera	6	Dryophilocoris flavoquadrimaculatus	174
Physocephela rufipes	6	Elasmucha grisea	85
Platycheirus granditarsus	130	Empicoris vagabundus	173
Procladius rufovittatus	156	Eurygaster testudinaria	9
Rhagio lineola	157	Gastrodes grossipes	173
Rhingia campestris	67	Gerris argentatus	195
Rivellia syngenesiae	184	Gerris odontogaster	118
Sargus bipunctatus	157	Graphocephala fennahi	86
Scathophaga stercoraria	110	Grypocoris stysi	118
Sepedon sphegea	184	Heterogaster urticae	85
Stomoxys calcitrans	110	Himacerus apterus	9
Stratiomys potamida	129	Hydrometra stagnorum	9
Tabanus bromius	157	Iassus lanio	174

Ilyocoris cimicoides	195	Cassinaria sp. (cocoon)	84
Ischnodemus sabuleti	194	Chrysis ignita	5
Macrosiphum rosae	174	Cimbex femorata	172
Macustus grisescens	119	Colletes cunicularius	141
Megalonotus chiragra	143	Colletes daviesanus	80
Metatropis rufescens	9	Collyria trichophthalma	171
Metopolophium dirhodum	86	Crossocerus megacephalus	82
Nabis limbatus	194	Crossocerus tarsatus	40
Neides tipularius	144	Cryptus armator	171
Neophilaenus campestris	144	Cryptus viduatorius	112
Neottiglossa pusilla	143	Cynips quercusfolii (galls)	16
Nepa cinerea	195	Diphyus quadripunctorius	192
Notonecta maculata	118	Diplazon laetatorius	83
Oncopsis flavicollis	9	Dolerus haematodes	84
Ovatus insistus	86	Dolerus triplicatus	172
Palomena prasina	85	Dolichovespula norwegica	82
Pantilius tunicatus	173	Dusona recta	111
Peritrechus lundii	143	Dusona recta (cocoon)	111
Physatocheila dumetorum	86	Earinus elator	111
Piezodorus lituratus	143	Elampus panzer	141
Pithanus maerkelii	144	Empria tridens	84
Plea minutissima	195	Euura bergmanni (larva)	193
Plocamaphis flocculosa	16	Euura poecilonota	84
Podops inuncta	143	Exephanes ischioxanthus	171
Psyllopsis fraxini	174	Formica fusca	5
Ranatra linearis	195	Formica rufa	170
Rhopalus subrufus	173	Gambrus carnifex	192
Tritomegas bicolor	118	Gelis aerator	192
Tuberolachnus salignus	195	Glypta fronticornis	171
Ulopa reticulata	144	Glypta monoceros	192
Zicrona caerulea	194	Glypta trochanterata	142
		Gorytes quadrifasciatus	141
Hymenoptera		Habrocampulum biguttatum	5
Aleiodes similis	84	Hepiopelmus melanogaster	83
Allantus calceatus (larva)	193	Ichneumon albiger	112
Amblyteles armatorius	142	Ichneumon gracilentus	171
Andrena flavipes	80	Ichneumon sarcitorius	83
Andrena fucata	111	Lasius flavus	141
Andrena haemorrhoa	80	Liposthenes glechomae	170
Apechthis compunctor	99	Lissonota biguttata	99
Apechthis rufata	51	Macrocentrus thoracicus	141
Apis melifera (comb)	81	Megachile centuncularis	80
Apis melifera (swarm)	81	Megachile willoughbiella	5
Arge pagana	112	Mellinus arvensis	170
Arge pagana (larva)	112	Mutilla europaea	5
Barylypa propugnator	171	Nematus alniastri (larva)	193
Bombus hypnorum	170	Nematus oligospilus	172
Bombus pascuorum	81	Netelia fuscicornis	142
Buathra laborator	14	Netelia testacea	100
Calameuta pallipes	5	Neuroterus quercusbaccarum	170
Caliroa cerasi (larva)	112	Nomada fabriciana	111

Favonius quercus (larva)	149	Pieris napi	180
Furcula furcula	93	Pleuroptya ruralis	97
Glyphipterix simpliciella	108	Poecilocampa populi	91
Gonepteryx rhamni	149	Polygonia c-album	105
Griposia aprilina	95	Polygonia c-album (larva)	105
Hadena compta	95	Polyommatus coridon	125
Hepialus humuli	90	Polyommatus icarus	8
Hipparchia semele	125	Pseudopanthera macularia	151
Hoffmannophila pseudospretella	66	Psyche casta (larva)	154
Korscheltellus lupulina	90	Pterophorus pentadactyla	97
Laspeyria flexula	94	Ptilodon capucina	152
Leucoma salicis (larva)	152	Ptilodon capucina (larva)	152
Lobesia reliquana	155	Pyrausta aurata	8
Lomaspilis marginata	152	Pyronia tithonus	105
Lomographa temerata	92	Saturnia pavonia	126
Lymantria monacha	153	Saturnia pavonia (larva)	18
Macroglossum stellatarum	91	Satyrium w-album	105
Malacosoma neustria	8	Satyrium w-album (larva)	105
Maniola jurtina	8	Scopula imitaria	107
Marasmarcha lunaedactyla	128	Scotopteryx bipunctaria	126
Melanargia galathea	125	Smerinthus ocellata	180
Menophra abruptaria	92	Spilosoma lubricipeda	93
Mesoleuca albicillata	150	Spilosoma lutea	93
Mesoleuca albicillata (larva)	150	Thera britannica	150
Miltochrista miniata	93	Thyatira batis	91
Mimas tiliae (larva)	66	Thymelicus lineola	125
Mompha locupletella	128	Tiliacea aurago	95
Morophaga choragella	154	Timandra comae	91
Nemophora degeerella	154	Tinea pellionella	66
Nola cucullatella	93	Tortrix viridana	96
Notocelia cynosbatella (larva)	108	Tyria jacobaeae	127
Notodonta dromedarius	152	Vanessa atalanta	65
Notodonta dromedarius (larva)	152	Vanessa atalanta (larva)	65
Nymphula nitidulata	181	Vanessa cardui	105
Ochropleura plecta	95	Watsonella binaria	91
Odontopera bidentata	151	Yoponomeuta padella	96
Operophtera brumata	107	Yponomeuta evonymella	108
Operophtera brumata (larva)	106	Ypsolopha dentella	96
Orgyia antiqua	107	Ypsolopha sequella	96
Orgyia antiqua (larva)	106	Zeuzera pyrina	8
Ourapteryx sambucaria	92	Zygaena filipendulae	8
Pammene regina	155	Zygaena trifolii	126
Pandemis corylana	155		
Parapoynx stratiotata	181	**Neuroptera**	
Parasemia plantaginis	153	Atlantoraphidia maculicollis	45
Pempelia palumbella	128	Conwentzia psociformis	87
Phalera bucephala	107	Crysopa perla	10
Phalera bucephala (larva)	106	Panorpa germanica	119
Pheosia gnoma	93	Sialis lutaria	196
Philedonides lunana	128	Sialis lutaria (larva)	17
Phlogophora meticulosa	153		

Odonata

Aeshna cyanea	88
Aeshna mixta	191
Calopteryx splendens	88
Calopteryx virgo	191
Ceriagrion tenellum	131
Coenagrion puella	88
Cordulegaster boltonii	131
Lestes sponsa	191
Leucorrhinia dubia	191
Libellula depressa	191
Orthetrum coerulescens	131
Pyrrhosoma nymphula	191
Sympetrum striolatum	10

Orthoptera

Conocephalus discolor	131
Conocephalus dorsalis	182
Leptophyes punctatissima	70
Meconema thalassinum	70
Metrioptera brachyptera	182
Pholidoptera griseoaptera	119
Stenobothrus lineatus	131
Tetrix ceperoi	10

Plecoptera

Isoperla grammatica	196

Psocoptera

Mesopsocus unipunctatus	175

Thysanoptera

Hoplothrips fungi	175

Thysanura

Petrobius maritimus	10

Trichoptera

Glyphotaelius pellucidus	182
Holocentropus picicornis	100
Limnephilus vittatus	182
Micropterna sequax	182
Mystacides azurea	182
Oecetis ochracea	100

Non-insect

Arctosa perita	11
Cornu aspersum	11
Lithobius variegatus	11
Neobisium carcinoides	29